Connoisseurs Choice

A pair of prancing horses hitched to this
1911 Rauch & Lang roadster would not seem
out of place. This is a transition car.
Powered by an electric engine, its coachwork
speaks of the past. Like other electric cars,
this one came equipped with a specially constructed rod, which could be looped over
trolley lines, thus recharging dead batteries
at no cost to the owner.

Connoisseurs Choice—

SELECTED BY BRIGGS S. CUNNINGHAM

PHOTOGRAPHS BY HENRY AUSTIN CLARK JR.

1912 HISPANO-SUIZA, ALFONSO XIII

RACING, SPORTS & TOURING CARS

TEXT BY JOHN W. BURGESS

A WALKER GALLERY BOOK
WALKER AND COMPANY • 720 FIFTH AVENUE • NEW YORK, N.Y. 10019

STAFF

EDITOR: Jozefa Stuart
ART DIRECTOR: Judith Woracek
MANAGING EDITOR: Andrea H. Curley
PRODUCTION: David Kellogg

FRONT COVER: 1932 STUTZ SUPER-BEARCAT DV-32
BACK COVER: 1929 MERCEDES-BENZ SSK

First published in the United States of America in 1979 by the Walker Publishing Company, Inc.

Published simultaneously in Canada by Beaverbooks, Limited, Pickering, Ontario.

Cloth   ISBN: 0-8027-0601-0
Paper   ISBN: 0-8027-7133-5

Library of Congress Catalog Card Number: 77-93729

Printed in Japan by Dai Nippon Printing Co., Ltd., Tokyo

10 9 8 7 6 5 4 3 2 1

With the exception of those listed below, all the photographs in this book are the work of Henry Austin Clark, Jr., of the Long Island Automotive Museum, Southampton, New York.

Page 4: courtesy John W. Burgess, photograph by Strother Macminn, Los Angeles, California

Pages 30, 34, 35: photographs by Peter Stevenson, Del Mar, California

Pages 71, 72: courtesy John W. Burgess, photographs by Jack W. Gilbert, Newport Beach, California

1927 GRAND PRIX 1.5-LITRE DELAGE

CONTENTS

BRIGGS CUNNINGHAM WITH HIS 1952 C-4R

INTRODUCTION

It is just under one hundred years ago that the first automobile, hesitantly, noisily but irrevocably made its first appearance. Since that time, in the mid-1880's, some 4,100 makes of cars have come and gone. In a fiercely competitive market, the survivors were few. It is sometimes hard for us today, who take the car so much for granted, to grasp the sheer wonder and excitement that the early automobile aroused. An amazing variety of cars came sputtering out of backroom bicycle shops, small iron foundries and householders' toolsheds. Whether they were powered by electricity, by steam or by the infant internal combustion engine, these early cars—so unlike our standardized models today—all had their own character and their own individuality. They did not roll easily off an assembly line but were carefully handcrafted and custom-built, from engine to coachwork.

A large part of the twentieth century's technological history lies tucked away under the hood of a Hispano-Suiza of 1913 or a Mercedes of 1914. And those who find the internal combustion engine of no great interest—or even an unfathomable mystery, can be enchanted by the historical charm of a Mercer Raceabout built in 1912 or the pure aesthetics of a Bentley of 1939. To assemble a truly first-rate collection of old cars, the collector must be part-engineer, part-historian and combine these attributes with an eye for aesthetics. The collection displayed at the Briggs Cunningham Automotive Museum in Costa Mesa, California, achieves a happy fusion of all three. A visit to the Cunningham collection serves as a reminder that cars can be glamorous and enthralling, that there are cars built to last, are a pleasure to drive and beautiful to look upon.

The Museum houses some one hundred cars. Of this number, forty are pictured in the following pages, in a range of make and time that stretches from a 1911 Rauch & Lang to a Ferrari of 1967, and encompasses the restrained elegance of a Rolls-Royce Silver Ghost to the fierce, battling lines of Briggs Cunningham's own racing machines built in the 1950's.

The Museum is the creation of Briggs Swift Cunningham and his wife, Laura. Over the years, both have formed close ties with the automobile racing world and the sports car in America. Mrs. Cunningham, who started drag racing at the age of 15, raced in many California events from 1952 to 1957 and became known, under the name Maxine Elmer, as the best woman driver in California. Briggs Cunningham, born in Cincinnati, Ohio, in 1907, was interested from early life on in many aspects of speed and competition. His first involvement, after he left Yale's Sheffield Scientific School, was with sailing. He raced his Six-Meter boat, the *Lulu*, and was a member of a Six-Meter U.S. team which defeated England. (Later he was to skipper the *Columbia*, which won the America's Cup Race in 1958.) He learned to fly a plane and, at the same time, he began to cultivate an interest in sports cars and road racing. While road racing was a popular and well-attended pastime in Europe, there was almost none in America in the 1930's. Nor were any sports cars being produced that could compete with racy little machines like the MG or the Alfa Romeo.

Through his friendship with three brothers, Miles, Sam and Barron, Jr., sons of a successful real estate and advertising man, Cunningham became part of a group of young men who dedicated themselves to the task of reviving road racing. Cunningham's initial contribution was to build a racing car, the hybrid Bu-Merc. It was a landmark native American sports car, built with the help of Charles Chayne, chief engineer of the Buick Company. The body was a Mercedes copy, the chassis a Buick. Cunningham gave it to his friend Miles Collier to drive in New York's 1940 World's Fair race. The car performed creditably during the race until it crashed into a lamp post.

During the war, Briggs Cunningham flew anti-submarine patrols for the Coast Guard. With war's end he was back in automobile racing. The cars he built for the 24-hour Le Mans race are discussed on page 58. While building racing cars, racing himself at Watkins Glen and many other American circuits, Cunningham also began to assemble the old cars that form the heart of the present collection. The first car he bought was the 1912 Mercer Raceabout; this was followed quickly by an American Underslung, of 1909, a 1913 Peugeot and one the most distinguished collections of Bentleys anywhere. He kept them licensed, tuned and ready to run on his Connecticut estate. By 1954 he owned somewhere between thirty and forty. In the early 1960's he moved to California and opened the Briggs Cunningham Automotive Museum.

Among automobile historians, this museum ranks among the best in the world. Anyone with money can amass what interests him, but it is the discerning and knowledgeable collector whose choice creates a valuable repository. Briggs Cunningham's selection of cars is never random. His expert eye and training have led him to choose cars that are, in one way or another, of special worth. From the 1913 Peugeot, the only model of this radical car still in existence, to that mammoth eccentricity designed by Ettore Bugatti, the "Royale", every car tells us something about the growth of the automobile. Sometimes a car's coachwork—its body—heralds future aesthetics, as is the case in the Hispano-Suizas in the collection. Or a car on display may incorporate an important technical advance; the Wills St. Claire, for instance, pioneered a cooling system and the first use of the metal molybdenum in an automobile. The Mercedes cars, the 1927 Delage, the jaunty pre-war MG K3 sports cars, the Bugatti T 55 are all cars that gained renown on the racing circuit, from the elite Grand Prix races to small local road tests.

As one connoisseur of old cars has observed: "This collection is truly the Louvre of the automobile world."

1952 C-4RK COUPE

THE 1913 PEUGEOT

If you are not familiar with the history of the automobile, you might easily assume that all there is to admire in this little Peugeot is its quaint, archaic charm. But any student of the development of cars knows better for—in its day—this car was a rebel, a radical departure from traditional engine design, and this Peugeot embodies ideas that were to leave their mark on engines for years to come.

This particular revolution was brought about by four solid and respectable men, working in near secrecy for the Peugeot Company at their factory in Lille, France. Although derided by their fellow workers for their radical ideas, who nicknamed them *Les Charlatans* (the quacks) and frowned upon by the conservative, business-oriented company management, the racing circuits of Europe and America soon proved they were right and their detractors wrong. Three of theese pioneers were racing drivers. All three knew from first-hand experience what was wrong with the racing cars of that time—they were large, top-heavy and cumbersome with an enormous engine capacity. But it was Ernest Henry, a Swiss engineer and the fourth member of this group, whose genius translated their practical ideas onto paper. To him goes the credit for designing the now-famous engine of the 1913 3-Litre Peugeot, which was to win the company so many races and consequently sell so many cars.

Almost as soon as the automobile emerged from its experimental cocoon, road racing began. At first, it was more a case of testing a car's endurance than its speed, but after the first real race in 1895—732 miles from Paris to Bordeaux and back—both Europe and the United States were afflicted with racing frenzy, a mania that included manufacturers, drivers and spectators, as well. Cars raced from city to city, over steep Alpine passes, on the sands of Florida and the winter ice of St. Petersburg's river. The roads were appalling. They were often mere cart ruts, from which rose dense clouds of dust that blinded the drivers, and flying stones that cut them. Fatalities were commonplace not only among the drivers but among the spectators, too. The machinery these early racing drivers handled was, to say the least, undependable—radiators punctured, the steering gear worked loose, pistons seized, to mention just a few of the endless ills that afflicted the early car.

What was the reason for this mania? In part it was the excitement of the new, in part the thrill of competition and in large part it sprang from commercial self-interest. For the makers of these early cars, winning or even surviving on those grueling road circuits was the best possible advertising. Cars that won sold. No matter how much a car was tested by the company, it was only in the competition with other marques that it could prove its worth to the buying public. The entire economy of many nations was changed by automobile sales and racing.

Furthermore, racing established itself early on as a useful seedbed for the development of the touring car. It forced improvements which could then be incorporated in more mundane vehicles.

Racing drivers were either professionals, usually members of a factory team, or gentleman amateurs, the wealthy sportsmen who gratefully accepted this new challenge to their skills—it

was more adventurous than stalking elephants in darkest Africa. In this country, for example, William K. Vanderbilt, after participating in some European racing, initiated the Vanderbilt Cup in 1904. By its third running in 1906 this race attracted a crowd of some 300,000. In Europe, the American owner of the Paris *Herald Tribune*, James Gordon Bennett, offered a trophy for an international, annual competition. The Gordon Bennett Cup was superceded in 1906 by France's first Grand Prix race, a race that was to set the future course for all racing.

Because racing was of such paramount importance to a car's builder, a curious—in fact, a dead-end—development occurred during the first decade of this century. Histories of the automobile refer to it as "The Age of the Monsters." The prototype cars built for a race increased to an alarming size; the designers and engineers equated performance with engine capacity. Cars of 13- and 15-litre capacity—some four times the size of a present-day family car—lumbered onto circuits, the huge engine encased in the lightest possible chassis in defiance of all safety considerations for the driver.

It was the engine designed by Ernest Henry and the three Peugeot racing drivers that brought The Age of the Monsters to a close. The engine they built in 1912 was based on a number of radical innovations which increased the performance of the car while decreasing its engine capacity.

The engine was the first to use a pent-roof combustion chamber and double overhead gearchain-driven camshafts with four valves per cylinder, which more accurately controlled the opening and closing of the intake and exhaust valves, rather like supplying the human body with an extra lung. Henry's new engine also included a ball-bearing crankshaft and a dry sump lubrication system, which used only a single pump for both scavenging and pressurizing the oil reservoir. Henry was among the first automobile designers to eliminate a gravity feed. He also improved the entire unit by installing a crankcase in a one-piece barrel shape with bolt-on ends and a center insert, thereby stiffened the whole engine. With a top speed of 95 m.p.h. and 105 horsepower, this Peugeot—made in a 7.6-litre and a 3-litre size—proved itself a formidable rival of other marques.

The following year the model, now in the Cunningham collection, competed at the Indianapolis Speedway in the classic Memorial Day race. At the wheel of Number 14 was the French driver Albert Buray, who had entered the race individually and was driving against the Peugeot factory team and their 5.65-Litre Peugeots. The 3-Litre Peugeot was by far the smallest car in the race. Duray, an expert and successful French driver, had borrowed it for this event from its owner, Jacques Meunier, son of France's Chocolate King.

The winner at the Speedway was a Delage, but Duray, to everyone's surprise, came in second, seven minutes behind the Delage after a driving time of 6 hours, 10 minutes and 24 seconds and an average speed of 80.09 m.p.h. ". . . the most striking feature of the race," wrote a contemporary reporter, "was the fact that the Duray Peugeot car finished second. . . . It was little less than a complete triumph for the small high-speed motor."*

The Automobile, Vol. XXX, No. 23, (New York: June 4, 1914).

FOLLOWING PAGES: 1913 GRAND PRIX 3-LITRE PEUGEOT

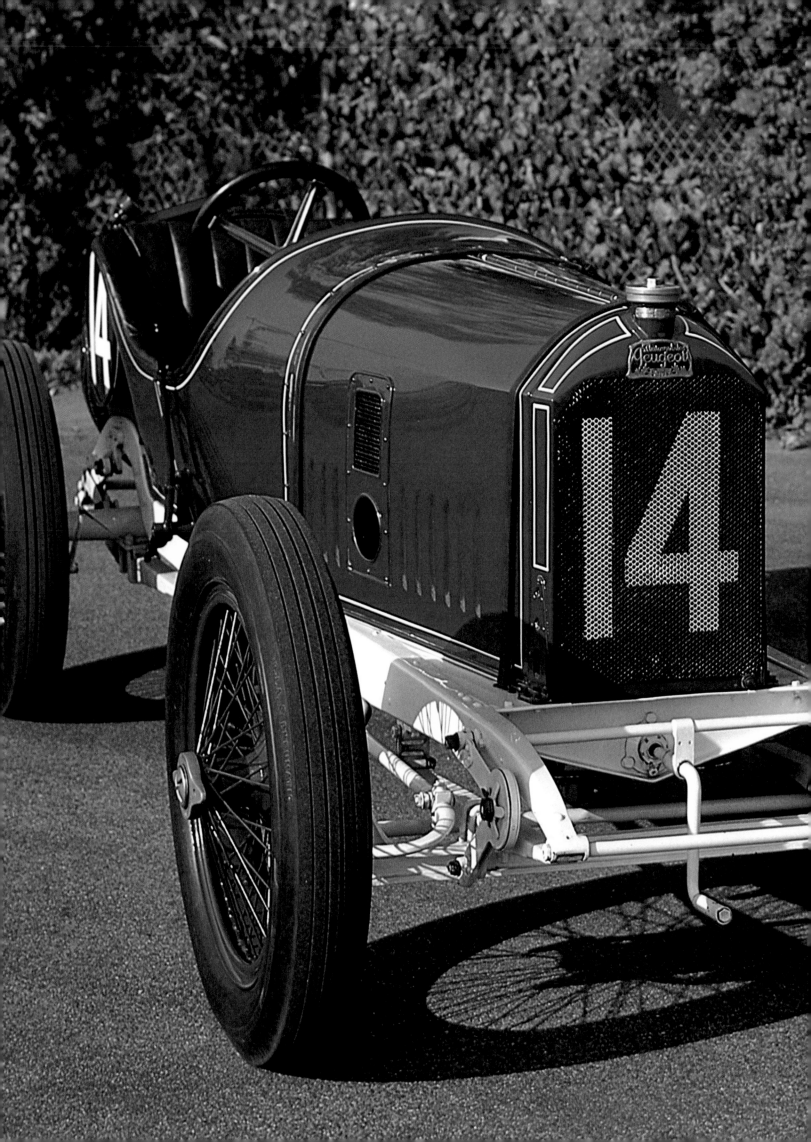

THE 1917 CUNNINGHAM

Harold Lloyd had one, so did Mary Pickford, Marshall Field and William Randolph Hearst. With such a roster of the rich and the famous, it is surprising that the Cunningham car isn't better known today. In fact, in its day, from 1907 until 1930 when production ceased, it was one of the best known of all American cars.

The car was built by the Cunningham brothers of Rochester, New York (no relation to Briggs Cunningham), who had been in the carriage trade since the mid-1800's. When they turned to making cars—at first simply buying engines and chassis components and assembling them—they continued an established tradition. The Cunningham car was never destined for the average purse; prices ranged from $6,500 to $9,000. Even after the firm began making its own cars in 1910, the automobile they built was custom-made, adapted to the individual client's desires.

The 1917 Cunningham in the Museum, driven by Ralph De Palma, was used to break many stock car records. Its V-8 engine has fully machined cylinder heads, a beautifully finished cast aluminum crankcase, timing case fan and a clever intake manifold, giving a downdraft effect with an updraft carburetor nestled between the cylinder banks.

1917 CUNNINGHAM

1912 MERCER "RACEABOUT"

THE 1912 MERCER

Mention the Mercer "Raceabout" to any lover of old cars and his eyes will mist and his voice soften. In the family of vintage cars, this is the best-beloved child. And with good reason. The car, first of all, is a delight to look upon—its unabashed sporting good looks and clean lines are unencumbered by gadgetry, yet adorned with handsome brass fittings. Secondly, the car was—and it still is—a joyous adventure to drive. From the time the Raceabout was first built, its 300-cubic-inch, 4-cylinder engine was capable of a speed of 80 m.p.h., scandalously fast for those pre-World War I years.

The Mercer was produced in Trenton, New Jersey (and named for Mercer County), by the Roebling family. But the credit for its enduring fame goes to the company's designer, Finlay Robertson Porter, who engineered and developed this two-seater sports car. Between 1911 and 1914 some five hundred Raceabouts were built and sold for about $2,500 each. In the general acclaim accorded this model, it is sometimes forgotten that the Roebling family also built touring cars and limousines, some of which were used as taxis, as well as furnishing the New Jersey State Police with speedy vehicles. But the Raceabout was the company's memorable car. Since it first came on the market, it has become one of the most sought-after, desirable collectors' cars in the world. Today a good Mercer Raceabout sells for a small fortune.

The Raceabout in the Cunningham collection is painted its original shade of blue, known as "Devil Blue", highlighted by restrained pinstriping. The car glows with enough burnished brasswork for a shipping magnate's yacht. It is the first old car acquired by Briggs Cunningham and one of the most admired in his collection. Moreover, now in its sixty-sixth year, it remains a pleasure to drive.

If the Raceabout had a technical weakness, it lay with its brakes. "The braking was poor," writes one sports car expert, G.N. Georgiano, "and emergency stops impossible—by the time the car had stopped, the emergency was twenty yards behind."* And, according to vintage car expert, the late Ken Purdy, who owned a Raceabout, "The brakes are pretty amusing, for example. . . . I used mine only for helpless old ladies with baby carriages, stalled freight trains and similar imperative necessities."* But chancy brakes did not deter dashing young bloods of Edwardian days.

Brakes aside, riding in a Mercer is an experience which brings to the driver and the passenger an appreciation of the early days of motoring. To begin with, the driver climbs into the right-hand, tight-fitting bucket seat, slips his right foot into a stirrup, which, placed outside the car's body, makes it possible for the driver to keep his foot braced and to operate the outboard-mounted accelerator. A bar on the dashboard serves as a brace for the left foot. Two hand-operated air pumps, one on the driver's side, the second on the passenger's, are used to supply fuel pressure until the air pressure in the gas tank has risen to 1½ to 2 pounds. Then the spark is retarded, the throttle set by levers on the steering wheel hub (a "Tee" handle between seats operates as the choke), the car cranked (usually the passenger's task), the ignition turned on and the ride begins.

It is not a ride for the comfort-prone. Driver and passenger are fully exposed to wind, rain or cold. But the car's light, accurate handling, its responsiveness to controls and the first-rate visibility it offers all combine to make a ride in a Raceabout exhilarating. Ken Purdy likened such a ride at high speeds to "the movement of a horse under you."

In those early days it was not unusual for a car to be picked up at a showroom, driven directly to a track, where the fenders and lights were usually removed for racing. After the race the car was driven home for the owner's personal use. Raceabout owners often did just that and the car achieved remarkable success at stock car races. *The Automobile Journal,* in an issue of October, 1912, lists Mercer cars as the number one winner of the year, with its rival and competitor, the Stutz "Bearcat", a close second. In that year, the Raceabout started eighty times; it finished in first place twenty-five times, in second place twenty-two times and came in third eighteen times. That same year, a Mercer finished third at the Indianapolis 500—a good showing for a small car that had six stops for tire changes and the misfortune to run out of gas in mid-race.

---

*G. N. Georgano, *A History of Sports Cars*, (New York: E. P. Dutton & Co. Inc., 1970), p. 56.

*Ken W. Purdy, *The Kings of the Road*, (New York: Bantam Books, 1954), p. 50.

1912 MERCER "RACEABOUT"

THE 1914 SIMPLEX

In the early days of the car business, Simplex was a much-favored trade name. This was, perhaps, an effort on the manufacturer's part to persuade potential customers that this new method of transportation was not, after all, so complex. Whatever the reason, the fact is that, from 1899 to 1914, the Dutch made a Simplex; Britain, in 1908, made the Simplex Perfecto; France made one equally briefly; and a Simplex steamcar was manufactured in Massachusetts from 1899 to 1901. But the Simplex that is still remembered and greatly treasured today is the car by that name which began life in Manhattan in 1904 and, in various guises, survived until 1924. Like its contemporaries, the Mercer Raceabout and the Stutz "Bearcat", this Simplex has gone down in American automotive history as one of the prime early sports cars.

At the turn of the century, Smith & Mabley of Manhattan imported expensive German Mercedes and French Panhards. The cost of these imports was high and included a 40% import tax. Furthermore, some of Smith & Mabley's customers were reluctant, even unwilling, to buy foreign cars. At that time, many Americans were eager to build up the fledgling native automobile industry. So the firm decided to produce their own car. They called it the Smith & Mabley Simplex. Although the original car was of a high quality, handsome to look at and painstakingly constructed, it owed a great deal to the Mercedes and lacked any technical innovations.

The firm set up its factory on East 83 Street, so the Simplex became the only car ever to be manufactured in Manhattan. There, under the supervision of designer Edward Franquist, the first cars were made. Enthusiastic owners began racing them immediately. Frank Croker, son of Boss Croker of Tammany Hall, raced in the opening Vanderbilt Cup of 1904 with no very distinguished results. At another race the following year, he overturned in his Simplex and was killed.

1907 was a financially depressed year and Smith & Mabley went bankrupt. The car survived. In the hands of its new owner, a banker named Herman Broesel, who dropped Smith & Mabley from the name, the Simplex very quickly developed into a popular roadster. Its success was helped by the enthusiastic support of Broesel's two Princeton sons and their Ivy League social circle. One collegiate friend entered his Simplex in every possible race with sufficient success for word spread that this was the car to own. The Simplex also did well in many major races and road tests. In 1908, at the first American Grand Prix held in Savannah, with racing driver Joe Seymour at the wheel, the Simplex made the best showing of any American entry. Against formidable European opposition—of the twenty entries, fourteen were from Europe—it came in ninth. In the same year and again the following year, a Simplex won the 24-hour Brighton Beach race.

Herman Broesel died in 1912 and his Simplex Automobile Co. was bought by a Wall Street firm, Lockhart, Goodrich and Smith. The Manhattan premises were closed and the firm moved to New Brunswick, New Jersey. Under the direction of a new engineer, Henry M. Crance, who took over from Edward Franquist, major production changes were made. He replaced the sports car with a magnificent touring car, which sold for about $10,000 and appealed to a group very different from the young bloods who had bought the sporting Simplex. The touring car was produced until 1917, at which time the company began to build Hispano-Suiza aero-engines for the war effort. After the war the company was sold again, to an ex-Packard salesman, and in 1924 went quietly out of business.

The Model F speedster in the Cunningham collection represents Edward Franquist's designing talents. The engine is a huge 4-cylinder with 2-cylinder "T" head blocks in groups of two each. It was the last passenger automobile in this country to use chain drive. Briggs Cunningham bought this car from the real estate and advertising magnate Barron Collier Jr. whose enthusiasm for road racing did so much in the 1930's to revive that sport in this country. The car came with chassis alone. The startling fire-engine red body it now displays is a direct replica—built by the Museum—of a 1914 Simplex illustrated in the company's catalogue. In an attempt to control the glare of night-time driving, the headlight lenses were fitted with visors, like those worn by a gambler at the tables. When this Simplex was first built, its chassis alone cost $4,000.

Displayed side by side in the Museum's showroom, the Simplex dwarfs its one-time rival, the Mercer Raceabout.

1914 SIMPLEX "SPEEDCAR"

THE 1915 PIERCE-ARROW

Luxury, reliability, elegance and, above all, quiet; these were the attributes of the cars made by the Pierce-Arrow Company of Buffalo, New York. In the years they were produced (from 1901 to 1938) prices ranged from $3,000 to $9,000; they were clearly intended for the affluent and the blue-bloods, destined to be driven on Fifth Avenue, Beacon Street and Newport Beach. On most Pierce-Arrows the chauffeur's speaking tube was installed as a matter of course and a few added the piquant detail of an umbrella or parasol holder. As a fitting expression of its conservatism, the company did not change from right-hand to left-hand drive until 1920.

George Nelson Pierce's company had begun, in 1860, with the manufacture of iceboxes and bird cages, advanced to bicycles, and from there to the automobile. In 1900, the company first tried out a steam car but it broke a rear axle on its initial test run and was thereafter discarded. Better luck followed with gasoline engines imported from France, and by the spring of 1901 the company had produced two finished models. These were called Motorettes, the diminutive justified by a weight of a mere 500 pounds and horsepower of 2¾. These tiny cars found a market, and within two years were being sold with double the horsepower.

Encouraged, the company moved onto ever heavier cars, producing a 4-cylinder, 28-horsepower monster, which cost the customer from $3,000 to $5,000.

The company's year of triumph was 1905. A Great Arrow —as the car was then still known—entered and won the first Glidden Tour Trophy, an endurance and reliability test, which was run from New York, through Hartford, Boston, Portsmouth, Bretton Woods and back. By trophy rules, each contestant began with 1,000 points; mechanical failure entailed loss of points. Mr. Pierce's car—driven by his son, with fiancee and parents along for the ride—finished the tour with a bal-

ance of 996 points and a vote by fellow contestants as the most outstanding entry. Other awards, here and in Europe, followed, among them four more Glidden Trophies. The company prospered accordingly. In 1909, for instance, orders for cars extended through 1911.

The 6-cylinder Model 48 was first produced in 1913, and its design incorporated headlights on the fenders, a distinctive Pierce-Arrow trademark of the future. But the car's greatest claim to distinction lies in the high quality of its workmanship, from the engine to the body. The cowl was beautifully made of cast aluminum sections riveted together. The instrument panel was designed to be aesthetically pleasing. Aluminum was also used for the crankcase, the oil pan, transmission housing and for the intake manifold. Water manifolds and fittings, as well as the cooling fan, were cast or fabricated in brass. The 6-cylinder engine of 8.5-litre capacity had three blocks of two cylinders each, cast as one, and integral heads with dual valves and dual ignition. All in all, the car stands as an example of automotive engineering at its best.

The 1915 Model, Series 3, in the Cunningham collection is a rumble-seat roadster. The occasional seat is fitted with a back rest, padded in leatherette, and folds up to leave a flush rear deck. The deep finish of this model is a conservative dark green with the fenders painted a complementary black.

Up to 1928, the Pierce-Arrow Company continued to produce 6-cylinder cars. (It was rumored, during the Prohibition years, that the quiet of a Pierce-Arrow engine made it popular among rum-runners.) But tastes changed and the market wanted multi-cylinder cars—eights and twelves. Despite refinancing and the production of multi-cylinder models, the company could not survive the Depression. In May of 1938, the Pierce-Arrow Company was sold at auction.

1915 PIERCE-ARROW

1915 PIERCE-ARROW

THE BUGATTIS

In his working lifetime, from the late 1890's to 1947, Ettore Bugatti created and produced some 7,500 cars of various kinds. Of this, between 1,880 and 1,900 have survived. In the special world of car collectors, the Bugatti is the elite car to own.

Many volumes have been written about Ettore Bugatti and his automobiles. For over forty years, the Bugatti Owners' Club—the oldest existing single marque club—has published a magazine. The whereabouts and the ownership of all remaining Bugattis have been catalogued. Why the fascination of this car above all others? The answer seems to lie in the aesthetic appeal of the car, combined with its superior performance. While not all automobiles created by Bugatti were perfect, they were all, like the man who designed them, characteristically individual.

A case in point is the "Royale" in the Cunningham Museum. It is unlike any other car ever built. From its conception to its execution, everything about it is outsize. Ettore Bugatti had already begun to dream about producing such a monster before the first World War. In April, 1913, he wrote to a friend that he intended to build a car which would be "extremely ex-pensive," larger than a Rolls-Royce or a Hispano-Siuza, yet lighter than either and, at a speed of some 93 m.p.h., run absolutely silently. ". . . this will certainly be," he wrote, "a vehicle and a piece of machinery beyond all criticism." Bugatti had to wait eleven years before he could start on his ambitious project. By 1927, the prototype was done and he was able to take W. F. Bradley, the correspondent for the English magazine *The Autocar*, for a country spin. "One might be excused for imaging that a car of this size and power [Bradley wrote] would have to be employed entirely on main highways. Probably M. Bugatti divined that this suspicion was lurking in our mind, for, on taking the car out, he quickly turned off the national highways and entered narrow, twisty hilly lanes with a particularly greasy surface. Further, for a considerable portion of the time he handled the car in that dashing manner which so much appeals to young bloods."

The car was not, of course, intended for young bloods. Bugatti designed it for royalty and hence its name.

The price of the car matched its exaggerated size. The chassis alone cost $25,000, with an additional $10,000 for the

body. The wheels stood waist high on a grown man, the wheelbase measured 170 inches, the engine capacity was 12.7 litres. Some automotive historians suspect that Bugatti found the car a useful housing for an engine he intended primarily for use in railcars. Certainly, "Royale" engines were later used to propel French trains.

The "Royale's" huge engine is a finely finished piece of machinery, in looks more like a hydro-electric plant than something found under the hood of a car. Although Bugatti followed his established engineering designs for this car, every part had to be scaled up in size and tools made expressly for its manufacture.

For such a giant the performance is livelier than one would expect. The accelerator responds quickly, the engine produces a great deal of usable torque and the outsize wheelbase and wheels erase all road bumps. Bugatti felt so certain of the reliability of his stupendous automobile that he guaranteed the chassis and the engine for the owner's lifetime, probably the only car ever to present such an offer. Even today, fifty years later, the steering on the car is precise and easy to handle. The car's top performance at sustained high speed over long distances must, however, remain a matter of conjecture. Who today would consider confronting the odds and driving such a unique and valuable car at top speed?

Only six Bugatti "Royales" were ever made—seven, counting the prototype car. Of the six, three were sold, none to a monarch. A Frenchman bought one car, a German another and an Englishman the third. The story goes that one eastern European monarch—possibly King Carol of Rumania—did try to buy a "Royale" but was rebuffed by Bugatti, who did not care for the king's table manners. The particular car in the Cunningham Museum is a two-door coupe, which was shown at the Paris Salon in 1932. During World War II, while still in the possession of the Bugatti family, the car was bricked up between two walls to avoid detection by the occupying Germans. In 1950 Briggs Cunningham bought it from Ettore Bugatti's daughter.

CONTINUED

1927 BUGATTI "ROYALE"

In complete contrast to the "Royale" and certainly more representative of Bugatti's work is the 1933 Supersports car in the Museum. This car, a Type 55, (all Bugattis are labelled with a type number just as they are all identifiable by their characteristic horseshoe-shaped radiators) has a supercharge 8-cylinder engine with a 2.3-litre capacity and a double overhead camshaft. This two-seater roadster's engine is based on the Type 51 Grand Prix engine, slightly detuned, and on the Type 54 Grand Prix chassis. It derives, therefore, from Ettore Bugatti's racing cars, his most masterly and successful creations. At one time, in the 1920's, within a space of four years, his racing cars won 1,851 times—a record that still stands.

1933 BUGATTI TYPE 55 SUPERSPORT

THE MERCEDES

While it is arguable whether or not the three-pointed star mounted on a thrusting prow is the best-known automobile emblem in the world, it is an indisputable historical fact that the Mercedes-Benz we drive today boasts the longest lineage of any automobile produced anywhere. In one form or another, these cars have been built since the mid-1880's. Until their merger in 1926, the Mercedes firm and the Benz firm were separate entities. Gottlieb Daimler designed and built the first Mercedes, Karl Benz the first Benz car. Both men have been credited — if such credit can be given to single individuals — with the invention of the automobile. Both were certainly pioneers in the field. Originally known as a Daimler, the Mercedes was renamed in 1900 to honor the daughter of a wealthy distributor of Daimler cars in France.

In the pre-war years, Benz and Daimler built a number of different cars — luxury models and, of course, racing machines. The Blitzen Benz in 1909 set a speed record, in a specially constructed model, of 124 m.p.h. A Mercedes won the French Grand Prix in 1908. Then, for five years, the firm dropped out of racing.

When the Mercedes cars again appeared at a race — the 1914 French Grand Prix run at Lyons — their newly designed machines won a staggering and dramatic victory. Five Mercedes cars were fielded and three of them took first, second and third place. Under the eyes of a disbelieving and sullen French crowd — Peugeots had won the last two Grand Prix races and were confidently expected to carry this one off, too — the Mercedes cars fought an epic battle over the 466-mile circuit against a Peugeot and won everything. Almost exactly four weeks later the first World War began. And almost at once the five Mercedes team cars (there was also a sixth car brought to the race but not run) attained international importance far beyond racing circles.

In the years shortly before 1914, with subsidy and encouragement from a bellicose German government, the Daimler firm, among others, experimented and built aero-engines. In 1913, Daimler was awarded the prize given by Kaiser Wilhelm for the most successful prototype. With the outbreak of war the French and British governments, under pressure to produce engines for their infant air forces, were eager to examine the successful Grand Prix engines for clues they might yield to the construction of the Daimler aero-engine.

1914 GRAND PRIX 4.5-LITRE MERCEDES

The Allied governments were in luck. Two of the team cars remained in France. One was sold to the American racing driver Ralph De Palma. And one other car—possibly the winning one—was sent to London to be displayed in the Mercedes showroom there.

Once war was declared the Rolls-Royce Company was assigned to produce aero-engines. With the gentlemanly proviso that they were not to examine the car as a whole, lest the company benefit commercially, the Rolls-Royce engineers were allowed by the British government to remove the Mercedes engine. As Alec Ulmann, the automotive engineer and historian of the Mercedes car, has written, "One can unmistakably see the Mercedes aero-engine construction of steel cylinders with welded-on water jackets in the overhead valve gear, which in a short space of time became the accepted construction for most of the Allied aircraft engines."* The Rolls-Royce Eagle and Falcon and France's Lorraine Dietrich all benefited from the Mercedes cylinder construction, which made for a lighter engine without loss of strength.

In the United States it was the design of the Liberty engine that exploited the Mercedes engine. Legend has it that several automobile experts locked themselves away in a hotel room in Washington D.C. and a few days later came up with a brand-new design for the Liberty engine. "Nothing could be a bigger exaggeration," writes Alec Ulmann. It is obvious that ". . . a copy of the German welded-up type of construction was made and, basically, the engine was an enlarged version of the Packard Model 3 that stemmed from the 1914 Lyons Grand Prix winner imported by De Palma."* Unfortunately, certain modifications of the original (single instead of dual intake and exhaust valves, for instance) weakened the Liberty engine and was to cause numerous engineering problems.

In 1914 the distributor for Mercedes in Belgium was one Andre Pilette, and he drove one of the team cars in the Grand Prix. This is the car that now stands in the Cunningham collection. With its 4-cylinder overhead cam engine of 115 horsepower, it is, to this day, a joy to drive. The front wheel brakes, while not used during the famous race, were used during practice runs. The steering is light, yet solid, a tribute to the engineering genius of the car's designer, Paul Daimler, son of the original builder of the Mercedes car.

*The Veteran Motor Car Club of America, Inc., *Bulb Horn*, Vol. XXXV, No. 6, (Boston: Nov.-Dec., 1974), p. 21 and p. 24.

1924 MERCEDES 28/95

1929 MERCEDES-BENZ SSK

1924 MERCEDES 28/95

This 1924 Mercedes in the Cunningham collection stands as a tribute to the energy and resourcefulness of the parent company. Within a remarkably short time after the defeat of Germany, and working under the stringent restrictions imposed on German industry by the victorious Allies, Mercedes cars were once again putting up a strong performance on racing circuits.

The 1924 Mercedes, produced for the general market, was identified by the name Targa Florio to capitalize on another and similar car's success in this notorious race.

The 7.25 model has a 6-cylinder engine with cast cylinders and light sheet metal welded water jackets. Two carburetors with beautifully balanced intake manifolds, made of brass, contribute to the outstanding quality of the engine.

Although the 28/95 was normally installed in a sedate touring car, it was also transformed into a two-seater roadster by the use of a short wheelbase chassis with a spartan aluminum body and fenders to help its performance. Riding in the occasional seat in the rear is a body-bruising experience for lack of suitable padding or any sort of consideration of creature comfort. This car was originally brought to the United States to be used at Indianapolis as a utility vehicle for the team. Only two cars of this exact model are known to be in this country.

1929 MERCEDES-BENZ SSK

The rakish lines, the suggestion of power conveyed by the exterior exhaust pipes and the length of the hood all combine to make this 7.1-litre two seater a symbol of the early sports car. It evokes a period when each make had its own individuality and a special value was put on sports cars. In its time the SSK was an outstanding and treasured automobile—and remains so to this day.

One of the greatest automotive engineers of all time, Ferdinand Porsche, came on the board of the Mercedes Company in 1924. Within three years, he had developed a 6-cylinder engine, out of which eventually grew the high speed SS and SSK models. Mercedes-Benz also produced, for racing only, the SSKL.

Although not built specifically for racing, certainly not for Grand Prix racing, both the SS and the SSK's competed successfully in countless sporting events. They won hill climbs, endurance tests and soon became the favorite roadster of prominent sportsmen.

The car in the Cunningham collection was originally custom-made for Dorothy Paget, one of England's foremost sportswomen. It was specially fitted with right-hand drive—the standard model had left-hand drive. An SSK is a rarity these days. Those that exist are in the hands of collectors. This car has been painstakingly restored by the Museum to its mint condition.

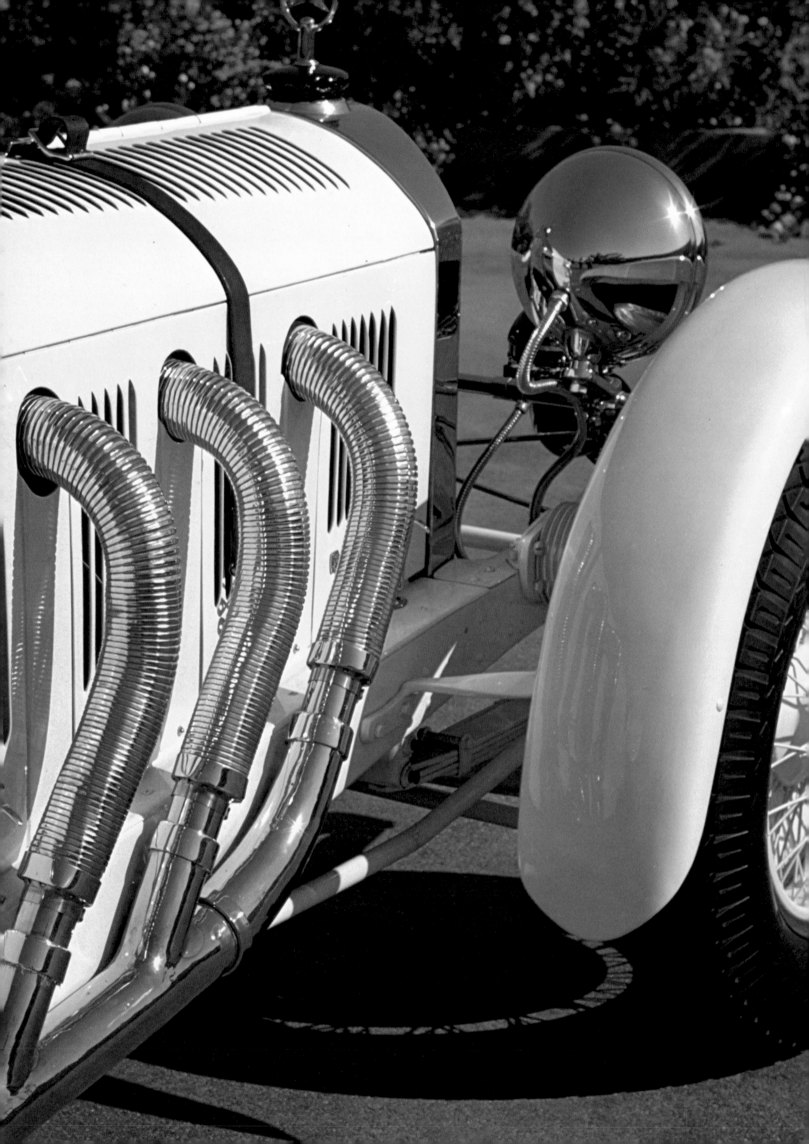

THE WILLS SAINTE CLAIRE

This handsome, two-seater roadster with a rumble seat was made by Childe Harold Wills. He named it after himself and Lake St. Claire, near his Michigan plant. Wills began his career with Henry Ford. He was the first engineer Ford hired and his first production manager. Wills invested in Ford, and when he left the company in 1919, he was a very rich man indeed. Determined to produce a high-quality car, he opened his own plant in 1921.

The model in the Cunningham collection is identified as A-68. The V-8 single overhead camshaft engine is in a class by itself among American-built automobiles. A solution to the critical cooling problem of V-8 engines (which exists to this day) was found by using a careful block and cylinder-head design, combined with an exactly laid-out water flow system. No water pumps were used or needed. Wills, who was also a metallurgist, introduced molybdenum into car manufacture. The Wills Sainte Claire is often known as the "molybdenum car." There is no doubt that the Wills engine is akin to the design of Marc Birkigt's Hispano-Suiza aero-engine. The car's emblem, a gray goose, may be Wills' bow of thanks to the Hispano's silver stork. Wills' last year of production was 1926.

1922 WILLS SAINTE CLAIRE

1929 MERCEDES-BENZ SSK

THE HISPANO-SUIZAS

When the first postwar Paris Salon for new automobiles opened in 1919, a British cartoonist, with commendable objectivity in view of the British Rolls-Royce on display, sat down and sketched the Hispano-Suiza entry. He titled his drawing: "Towering Above All Others." In so doing, he expressed the sentiment and the belief of many—both then and now.

The story of the Hispano-Suiza is in truth the story of the man who conceived this car from its inception in 1904 to its final model in 1944. Marc Birkigt, a Swiss engineer, was a graduate of the acclaimed Ecole des Arts and des Metiers in Geneva. Birkigt was an engineer of genius, paramount among his peers, who combined immense technical talents with an innate sense of beauty, a drive for perfection and a limitless love of hard work.

Birkigt came to Barcelona, Spain, in the year 1899 to work on the manufacture of electrical buses. Soon thereafter he was working with a small firm making a 20-horsepower car called the Castro. La Fábrica de Automoviles la Hispano-Suiza was formed in 1904 with Spanish financing allied to Swiss genius. The first car produced was merely the Castro renamed, but by 1907, true Birkigt creations were being sold. And, fortuitously, the car caught the eye of the Spanish monarch, King Alfonso XIII, who loved to don goggles and driving helmet and take the wheel himself. His majesty gave the car his royal endorsement.

Under this patronage the firm flourished. The cars were called the Alfonso XIII and quickly became the special preserve of the well-born and stylish, and their imitators, the new-rich. This car is nowadays considered to be the forerunner of the light, precise and responsive European sports car. Its relatively small 4-cylinder engine yielded a healthy 64 horsepower and, when race-tuned, could reach 90 m.p.h. The design was a personal triumph for Birkigt, one of many to come. Among his many contributions to automobile engineering, a few of the most outstanding are the first use of a monobloc engine, the first supercharger and high-turning engines.

Although the Hispano-Suiza firm itself was never especially enthusiastic about racing, this was not true of the sports-minded owners of the car. The first race won by a Hispano-Suiza was the Coupe de L'Auto (the small car Grand Prix race) of 1910. The following year, this car was put into production—with a slightly larger engine—and the Queen of Spain

CONTINUED

presented her "august husband" with one. This became the Alfonso XIII model. France, Germany and England were more advanced in the automobile world at that time than Spain and furnished a much richer market for cars. This fact made the Hispano-Suiza largely an export car. Whether on economic grounds or as a matter of convenience, the firm opened a plant on the outskirts of Paris in 1911. It was originally intended purely for the assembly of parts, but after the war it grew into a full-production center. More and more, the Hispano-Suiza came to be looked upon as a French rather than a Spanish car and as such it has gone down in history.

The 1912 Alfonso XIII in the Cunningham collection is one of the Museum's most prized automobiles, an exceptional example of an early masterpiece by the gifted Marc Birkigt.

In 1914, when war came and automobile production ceased, one of the most remarkable achievements of Birkigt's career took its place. The aero-engine he designed powered more than 50,000 World War I pursuit planes. They were flown by all the famous Allied aces from the RAF's Billy Bishop—who shot down seventy-two enemy aircraft—to the Frenchman Rene Fonck with seventy-five to his credit. This aero-engine was manufactured in every Allied country, including the United States, and after the war became the basis of Hispano-Suiza's fabled new line of luxury cars. The graceful silver stork, which emblazoned the hood of every car after 1918, was adopted to honor the fallen French ace Capitaine Georges Guynemer, whose symbol it had been.

It was this car that overwhelmed the crowd at the 1919 Paris Salon. The 6 cylinders were made of aluminum with steel liners, a single overhead camshaft operated two valves for each cylinder, the engine produced 135 horsepower, the chassis was strong but light. It had four-wheel servo-brakes, unusual at that time. The car was the essence of reliability in its performance, as befitted an automobile destined for the rich.

The Hispano-Suiza was an overnight success. The 1924 best-selling novel by Michael Arlen, *The Green Hat*, contains a description of a Hispano-Suiza that conveys the admiration felt for the car at that time. "This car charmed the eye," the author wrote, "like a huge yellow insect that had dropped to earth from a butterfly civilization, this car, gallant and suave, rested in the lowly silence of the Shepherd's Market night. Open as a yacht, it wore a great shining bonnet and flying over the crest of this bonnet, as though in proud flight over the scores of phantom horses, was that stork by which the gentle may be pleased to know that they have just escaped death beneath the wheels of a Hispano-Suiza car. . . ."*

Although this car was first and foremost a luxury tourer, it was also adaptable to racing. In 1921, for instance, Andre Dubonnet, of aperitif fame, entered his 8-litre, 6-cylinder roadster in the Targa Florio. Although the car came in fifth, it nevertheless proved its ability in this most demanding of all races to stay the course. The firm itself then entered racing, fielding a 6-cylinder car with a slightly heavier chassis than the production model. The factory team won the Boillot Cup three times. Because the race was held in Boulogne, one line of the marque was henceforth known as the Boulogne.

The car in the Cunningham collection may well be a Boulogne model, of which only fifteen were produced. It is a boattail speedster with sensitively designed flared fenders. The quality of the engine is exemplified in the owner's handbook, which notes that "on starting on level ground one should start off in second gear, shifting into third to obtain the desired top speed." Low gear is not mentioned for normal driving.

The story of the discovery of this particular Hispano-Suiza reads like the wish-fulfillment dreams of all dedicated old car collectors. Driving through Pennsylvania one day in 1954—in a Mercer, of course—the noted collector Alec Ulmann stopped for gas in a very small place named Black Eddy. As is the habit of such devotees, he asked the attendant if there were any interesting old automobiles around the neighborhood. "Only an old La Salle," was the answer. An old La Salle was of no interest to Mr. Ulmann, but the attendant went on to mention, casually, that this model had right-hand drive. "I knew at once what it was," Mr. Ulmann recollects today. "La Salles were copies of the old Hispanos." He left his Mercer at the garage—no astute car collector ever goes hunting in an old car, it is too much of a giveaway—and he walked over to the farm where the car reputedly was. It was, indeed, a Hispano—year 1928—and he bought it for $300.00. He now believes that it had probably been abandoned by careless, wasteful summer people.

Meticulous shop work at the Museum restored the car, right down to the last chassis bolt, and also renewed the smooth gloss of the panels and the glistening bodywork by the coachmaker Kellner. And interesting sidelight, which upholds the Hispano-Suiza tradition of excellence, was the discovery by the Museum staff that, even after a long and eventful life, the differential of the car showed less slack between gears than is found in many cars rolling off the assembly line today.

---

*Michael Arlen, *The Green Hat*, (New York: George H. Doran Co., 1924), pp. 15-16.

1928 HISPANO-SUIZA "BOULOGNE" CHASSIS

THE 1927 VAUXHALL

In his autobiography, *Great Morning*, Osbert Sitwell recalls the exultation experienced by the youth of the turn of the century when driving an open car. "This vehicle, so modern and of its time, induced in the young man a sense of being heir of all the ages, lord of all he passed by. . . . The open car belonged to that day. No other generation had been able to speed into the sunset."*

It was for young men such as these that the Vauxhall Iron Works Ltd. of England produced their open Prince Henry model. Like many another firm, Vauxhall also made tourers,

---

*Richard Hough, ed., *The Motor Car Lover's Companion*, (New York: Harper & Row, 1965), p. 16.

designed to carry the sedate and the staid safely through their daily rounds. But it is the jauntier car, forebear of the 1920's sports car, that is remembered. With the minimum of protection, and very often with no doors, it allowed its driver to relish to the full the sensation of rushing through the countryside.

The original Prince Henry model had a 3-litre engine and was entered in the 1910 Prince Henry of Prussia Trials. These Trials, organized by Prince Henry, younger brother of Kaiser William, lasted a week, covered between 1,200 and 1,500 miles. Any kind of a showing in them constituted superb advertising. While the Vauxhall did nowhere near as well as a rival Daimler (Mercedes-to-be), the car did go through the whole lengthy course without a breakdown. This was enough to achieve instant recognition. To exploit this, the company's

1911 open car, now 4 litres, was named the Prince Henry. With a 6-cylinder engine, it was capable of a top speed of 75 m.p.h., sufficient to satisfy the thirst for speed in any young man.

Then in 1913, shortly before the outbreak of war, Vauxhall offered yet another open car, mundanely designated as the E 30/98. Out of this car grew the OE 30/98, which many consider the greatest sports car of the 1920's.

The 1927 Vauxhall in the Cunningham collection is an outstanding example of an OE 30/98. Described by Vauxhall as a fast, light touring car, it is apparent that the designer was loath to exclude details that would make the car competition-worthy. The fenders, for instance, are detachable. The monstrous exhaust pipes and the rugged look of the controls are all competition touches. Private owners in the '20's did, in fact, race

their Vauxhalls in smaller races and hill climbs throughout England and the Continent.

The 4-cylinder, overhead valve engine produces 120 horsepower, but the Cunningham model has been modified to improve on this. Vauxhall brakes were notoriously quirky, so this car was fitted with hydraulic brakes when it took part in sports car road events in this country during the 1940's.

The car's aluminum polished body glows like old pewter; its gleaming chrome and rich nickel silver hold the light. This car's striking good looks, allied to its performance on the road, make this OE 30/98 the essence of the vintage sports car.

In 1926 General Motors bought the Vauxhall Iron Works. Two years later the OE 30/98 was no longer in production.

1922 VAUXHALL

THE STUTZES

1929 STUTZ FOUR-PASSENGER SPEEDS[...]

Once upon a time, some 75 years ago, a young farm boy left the open fields of Ohio for the machine shops of Indianapolis. He was Harry C. Stutz and he gave his name to a car that has since become a legend. He began making cars in 1909, and the very first he ever produced came in seventh at the year's Indianapolis 500, a good enough showing for that confident promoter, Harry Stutz, to advertise his product as "The Car That Made Good in a Day."

Success followed success on racing circuits throughout the country, and in 1914 Stutz produced his first Bearcat, modelled on his victorious racing cars. It was a 4- or 6-cylinder car, designed to appeal to a sports clientele. Although the car was in production up to the early 1920's, later models were much more sedate. Any hip-flask-carrying young man of the Roaring Twenties who possessed a Bearcat was probably driving a second-hand car.

Harry Stutz left the company in 1919 on the heels of a disastrously mismanaged financial expansion. Charles Schwab of Bethlehem Steel took it over and put Frederic Ewan Moskovics, a seasoned automotive engineer, in charge. He at once changed the company's image and set about producing a line of luxury touring cars. The first of these, the Safety Stutz, appeared in 1926.

The 1929 model in the Cunningham collection has a rakish body designed by LeBaron. More than most cars of the time, the low chassis gave the car a road-hugging appearance and generally the look of a racing car, which was enhanced by the raked front and rear cockpit windshields, the cut-down doors and the style of the front cockpit itself. All in all, the car gave an impression of speed wedded to creature comforts. The overhead valve straight-8 engine has a displacement of 332 cubic inches and 115 horsepower. In its day, this car was accepted as one of America's finest sports cars.

In 1932, to boost flagging sales, the firm brought out the Super-Bearcat—the DV-32—in an effort to capitalize on its great past. It was a powerful automobile with an advanced double overhead camshaft, straight-8 engine with four valves per cylinder, capable of 156 horsepower. In performance and in looks, this light-weight roadster echoed the original Bearcat. Up to the end of the 1950's, the engines of the DV-32 were still being installed in Stutz specials and competed in road racing.

Long before that, the Depression had taken its toll of this famous make, and in 1937 the Stutz Company closed its doors.

1932 STUTZ SUPER-BEARCAT DV-32

THE 1927 DELAGE

Everything that a racing car should be is embodied in the 1927 Delage. Its clean, sweeping lines, the low drop of the body and the classically sculptured cowling speak of speed joined with aesthetics. The car's supercharged engine resembles a gigantic and meticulously crafted watch that will never lose time. Like a jewelled movement, every part of the machinery that turns is set in fine ball and roller bearings. When this car took to the racing circuit, its craftsmanship bore fruit in a series of victories. It overwhelmed all opposition—including Ettore Bugatti's world-renowned models.

The car bears the name of the owner of the company, Louis Delage; but credit for its creation and its performance must go to two engineers, Albert Lory and Maurice Gauthier, although Delage himself, a shrewd businessman, had had an early appreciation of the promotional value of racing.

Louis Delage began building cars in France in 1905, and by 1906 he was already in the business of racing, while continuing to produce touring models. As with other marques, success on the circuit brought success in the salesroom. Very soon Delage was a wealthy man and grew even more so during the first World War when his plant manufactured munitions. An ambitious man, he bought a chateau, a yacht, a Parisian townhouse and opened a luxurious showroom on the Champs

Elysees. But despite displays of wealth, Delage had been trained as an engineer and knew enough to understand that he had to employ the best in the field to maintain his position. His personal motto, Make one thing but make it well *(Faire qu'une chose mais la bien faire)*, is reflected in the quality of the cars he produced. Delage cars, aimed at the luxury market, were always striking in appearance with particularly distinguished bodywork. Throughout the pre-war years and in the 1920's, his firm prospered. But the worldwide depression of the 1930's destroyed him. His business was taken over by the Delahaye Company; he lost his personal fortune and died a poor man in 1947.

The greatest car he ever built was, without doubt, the 1.5-Litre Grand Prix car, which won him so much acclaim in racing circles. Four years after the end of the war Delage was busy producing racing cars; by 1925 his 2-litre cars won the French and the Spanish Grand Prix. In 1926, the 1.5-litre supercharged car made its initial appearance at the European Grand Prix. This race was nothing more nor less than a personal combat between the Bugattis and the Delages; no other marques participated. A Bugatti came in first and third, a Delage placed second. What probably cost the Delage first place was a basic, elementary oversight on the part of Albert

1927 GRAND PRIX 1.5-LITRE DELAGE

Lory. The twin superchargers had been placed on the near side of the engine so that the opposite exhaust came so close to the accelerator pedal that it grew red hot when the car was running. These cars, writes William Court, historian of Grand Prix racing, "contrived to give their drivers a shattering foretaste of the flames of hell-fire."* This race, run in 110 degree heat, took place in July. Just three weeks later, with time for only minor modifications, the Delage team participated in the British Grand Prix, run at Brooklands. From time to time throughout the race, spectators watched the Delage drivers jump from their cars to plunge their feet into pans of cold water. Despite these delays, the race was a victory for the Delage. One of many to come.

By 1927 Lory had rectified his mistakes. The car Delage brought to the Grand Prix circuits that year was perfect in every respect: it was a joy to look upon, its performance was unsurpassed, it was fast, it was—for its day—quiet and it proved to be one of the most reliable cars ever built.

The Delage offered so great a threat that even the confident

---
*William Court, *A History of Grand Prix Racing, 1906–1951, Power and Glory*, (London: Macdonald, 1966), p. 150.

Ettore Bugatti wisely withdrew his team; "I am beaten—my cars cannot win the race," he said. That year, the Delage carried off all the major prizes, winning the French, the Spanish, the British and the European Grand Prix at Monza. Satisfied with this success, Delage then retired the 1.5-Litre from the racing circuit. Exactly nine years later, in private hands, it won four straight Grand Prix races again, without the necessity of tearing down the engine after the third race. Automotive experts consider this feat an all-time sensational performance and liken it to winning the Indianapolis 500 three times before an engine overhaul.

In 1929 Louis Chiron brought a 1.5-Litre Delage to Indianapolis. Because he did not know the course, he only finished seventh, a good showing under the circumstances. It is this particular car that is now in the Cunningham collection. As small in displacement as most Volkswagen engines, this car can still produce, forty years later, 170 horsepower, pushing the 1800-pound car to a top speed of 128 m.p.h. Not many of these superb cars were made and very few survived the years. Due to their extraordinary performance, these Delages became racing favorites with the result that many were destroyed. Only two actually survived into the late 1960's. One of these burnt, and has been rebuilt. So the only true original is the car in the Cunningham collection today.

THE ROLLS-ROYCES

The Honorable Charles Stewart Rolls, third son of Lord Llangattock, provided the glamor and the frills. Mr. Frederick Henry Royce, a working-class Manchester manufacturer, supplied superlative craftsmanship and a stern dedication to hard work. And Mr. Claude Goodman Johnson, a London businessman, brought commercial acumen and promotional flair. Between them, in 1904, they launched Rolls-Royce Ltd., destined to grow into one of the most successful and enduring automobile companies ever established.

Rolls, rich and well born, typified the aristocrat's enthusiasm for the new, fast machinery of the time. He flew aeroplanes, he raced cars, he investigated balloon flights. On the side, he imported and sold the French Panhard car and the Belgian Minerva. Claude Johnson partnered him. Royce emerged from extreme poverty—he was a newsboy and errand boy in his teens—to the ownership of a company that made heavy electrical equipment. At the age of forty, dissatisfied with the performance of a 2-cylinder Decauville he owned, Royce decided he could build a better car himself. He built three in his factory and the whole story might have ended there, had not Rolls in London thought of acquiring a British car to sell. Someone mentioned Royce's three cars. Thus was born Rolls-Royce Ltd.

By 1905 the first car was on display in London. By 1907 a 6-cylinder model appeared on the market. Johnson, ever the imaginative promoter, took the thirteenth chassis of this model, clothed it in aluminum and silver-plated hardware with a plaque on the dashboard inscribed: Silver Ghost. The publicity was brilliant, for the name implied one of the Rolls-Royce's chief selling points—the noiseless engine. Many of Rolls-Royces' future names, from Phantom to Wraith, echo Mr. Johnson's original inspiration.

Johnson did much more than rely on a catchy name to make the car known. Under the critical eye of the Royal Automobile Club, the Silver Ghost drove 2,000 miles, charting the course for the Scottish Trials. It then participated in the Trials, racking up another 1,500 miles. At the same time it was decided that henceforth Rolls-Royce would only produce one model. All models predating the Silver Ghost were taken out of production.

Altogether, one hundred seventy-three Silver Ghosts were made. It was the car that made the Rolls-Royce name synonymous with understated elegance, reliability, quiet and durability. During the first World War its engines powered armored cars. T. E. Lawrence gave the engine of the Silver Ghost a further boost when he used the car to hound Turks across the deserts of Arabia. The Silver Ghost is rumored to have reappeared twenty-five years later—in the desert warfare of World War II.

The 1914 Silver Ghost in the Cunningham collection reflects all the straightforward quality that created the Rolls-Royce image. Its simple, finely constructed 6-cylinder, 7.4-litre engine can be stopped and then re-started on the compression left in the cylinders. It does this so smoothly that, even with the hood up, it is barely possible to tell that the engine is in fact turning again. This model is a four-passenger tourer with a body built by the Parisian coachworker Kellner. (Not until 1951 did Rolls-Royce supply bodies with its chassis.) Today a car like the Silver Ghost is looked upon as an extravagant and magnificent automobile intended for the Edwardian equivalent of the Jet Set. In actual fact, the main market for the Silver Ghost was found among England's self-assured, conservative land-owning class, the country gentry. It was not meant to appeal to the flamboyantly rich but to people who had no interest in self-advertisment or in flaunting their wealth, those who, instead, sought quiet and dependability. The Silver Ghost was made in their image.

In 1910, at the Bournemouth air meet, Charles Rolls was killed in a crash, the first Briton to meet such a death. By this time his interest in automobiles had already begun to wane and he may, in fact, have already sold out his share in the Rolls-Royce Company. His death had little effect on the fortunes of Rolls-Royce Ltd.

After four years of war production, Rolls-Royce returned to the Silver Ghost. In 1919 Johnson set up a subsidiary in Massachusetts, which was to produce cars for the American market and avoid the import tax. It would also make cars with left-hand drive and a central change. This venture lasted twelve years. It became apparent that part of the snob value of a Rolls-Royce lay in its foreign origin. Those who could afford a Rolls-Royce—the chassis alone cost $11,750—sought the cachet of buying abroad.

The Silver Ghost faded away in 1925 to be replaced by the Phantom I, which was to last four years in England, two more in the United States. In its place materialized the Phantom II. The first Phantom's engine was a somewhat more powerful version of the Silver Ghost. It had overhead rather than side valves. Although the Rolls-Royce resolutely refuses to release horsepower statistics, it has been estimated that this car had around one hundred. The engine of the Phantom II once again stepped up the car's power capability although the company was careful to point out that the car "is not intended to compete with racing or ultra-sporting types. . . . " It was a tourer for people who liked to go fast. Its engine was a highly refined 6-cylinders, with overhead valves, pushrod operated with detachable aluminum cylinder heads.

The 1931 model in the Cunningham Museum has a roadster body built by the well-known coachmaker James Young of Bromley. It was originally owned by a lady known for her great interest in sports and the left side of the rear compartment has storage room for golf clubs. Fold-down steps facilitate access to the rumble seat in the rear flush deck. The interior is upholstered in brown leather and the body is painted a rich, emerald green lacquer.

CONTINUED

1914 ROLLS-ROYCE SILVER GHOST

1936 ROLLS-ROYCE PHANTOM III

1931 ROLLS-ROYCE PHANTOM II

Unlike so many makes of expensive cars, the Rolls-Royce rode through the Depression scarcely feeling the bumps. Henry (now Sir Henry) Royce died in 1931. He had been a sick man for twenty years and spent them in his villa in the south of France or at his English country house. Although absent from the plant, he ran it with iron discipline from a distance. Royce was a sunrise-to-sunset-and-beyond worker, including weekends. Overwork had caused his illness as it had brought about the death of Claude Johnson in 1926. Royce's only diversion was his garden, in which he had had night lighting installed so that he could work after dark. He was never one of the great theoretical engineers of his day and could not match men of the caliber of Mark Birkigt or Ernst Henry. It has been said that he could not even use a slide rule. However, he was, par excellence, the master mechanic, who understood engine components with instinctive insight and a drive for perfection. Shoddy work or carelessness among his workers could fire up a towering rage in Royce. He had his steel made specially, every engine component was tested and re-tested. This care brought fruit. It has been estimated that almost 50% of all Rolls-Royce cars ever constructed have survived the years.

The car came with a three-year owner's guarantee, a fact which has led to one of the most often-told anecdotes about the company. The locale of the story is set anywhere from the Pyrenees to the Himalayas, the relevant breakdown can be a rear axle or a drive shaft. But the message the story tells never varies. A part breaks down. The owner cables to England for a replacement. A mechanic flies out bringing the needed part and repairs the car. Subsequently, the grateful owner, back in England, visits the Rolls-Royce offices to tender his thanks and pay his bill. To his astonishment, no one at the office has ever heard of him, of his car, of a breakdown and, finally, of a mechanic flying to foreign parts with a replacement. The dumbfounded owner finally understands: Rolls-Royce parts do not break down.

The Phantom III was shown at Olympia, London's answer to the Paris Salon, in 1935. It is the company's first 12-cylinder automobile and the first to have independent suspension. The engine, with a displacement of 448 cubic inches, is a 60° V-12 with pushrod-operated overhead valves.

Both the Phantom III's in the Cunningham collection have extravagantly appointed interiors, as befits a Rolls-Royce of that era. The 1936 model, whose body was built for Barbara Hutton, Woolworth heiress, is luxuriously upholstered in leather. A recessed telephone in the rear conveyed orders to the chauffeur or footman, who sat in front of a glass panel. The quiet, understated body is the work of Saoutchik. Miss Hutton gave the car to her racing driver son, the late Lance Reventlow, who installed excellent power steering and had the car painted a deep, sensual chocolate brown.

The 1937 Phantom III was a slightly worn limousine when Briggs Cunningham acquired it. The well-known body builder Mulliner transformed it into a luxurious but restrained four-door saloon, its interior fitted out with gray leather upholstery and matching gray carpeting.

1937 ROLLS-ROYCE PHANTOM III

THE BENTLEYS

At the outset, it is best to understand that the history of the Bentley car is composed of two distinct chapters. The first chapter tells the story of the Bentley as it was from 1919 to 1931, the years when W. O. Bentley himself designed and built his legendary sports cars. The second chapter begins in 1931, when Rolls-Royce Ltd. acquired Bentley's bankrupt firm and changed the character of the car to conform with its own.

Walter Owen Bentley is a controversial figure in automobile engineering history. Fiercely revered by many—especially in his native England—he is disparaged by some, who claim that his designs relied on brute strength, rather than engineering subtleties, to power his cars. On the other hand, Bentley fans are in a strong position for they can cite documentary evidence. In the 1920's the Bentleys totaled a noteworthy number of wins at road races across Europe as well as in Great Britain. Between 1923 and 1930 Bentleys placed first five times at the Le Mans 24-hour endurance race. In addition, in 1928, the 4.5-Litre Bentley established a world's record of 200 miles at 110.26 miles per hour. Bentleys and speed became synonymous. Many years after they were no longer made, James Bond, in Ian Fleming's novel *Moonraker*, pursues the villain in a twenty-five-year-old, supercharged 4.5-Litre Bentley equipped with a concealed gun holster.

W. O. Bentley began his working life as an apprentice for the Great Northern Railway. While he worked there he acquired a 2-cylinder motorcycle, which he entered in the London-Edinburgh Reliability Trial and won a gold medal. In 1912 he formed a partnership with his brother to import and sell French cars. He began with three marques but quickly discarded two as inferior. He remained with the D.F.P. (Doriot, Flandrin et Parant) which, although its 4-cylinder single camshaft engine was not a brilliant performer, allowed for modification. To advertise the car Bentley entered his modified model in hill climbs and road races at which the car did well.

Once on a visit to D.F.P. in Paris, Bentley came across a toy, a miniature piston made of aluminum. He took the toy back to England and ordered a set of pistons for his D.F.P. made of 88% aluminum and 12% copper alloy. Once installed in his car, he found that these tougher pistons augmented its speed to 89.70 m.p.h. In the Isle of Man Tourist Trophy of 1914, competing against cars specifically designed for racing, Bentley in his passenger automobile came in sixth.

When war broke out Bentley went to work on aero-engines, into whose design he incorporated what he had learned from his car. His aero-engines, the Bentley Rotary I and II, used

aluminum pistons as well as steel-lined aluminum cylinders. By the end of the war, his engines had proved themselves. One of their great advantages in combat stemmed from their ability to attain increased altitudes.

As soon as the war was over, Bentley returned to automobiles, this time as a designer and manufacturer. His first car, powered by a 3-litre engine, won at Le Mans in 1924 and 1927. In 1922 it took second, third and fifth places in the English Tourist Trophy races.

Bentley built his car for reliability as well as for speed. To achieve the first he made a heavy chassis, and for the second, a powerful engine. In doing so, he went against the convention held by most designers of that day who believed that sports cars should be small and light.

The 3-litre model in the Museum has a particularly fetching body, with a wooden deck on the boattail section and a fabric-covered body, custom-designed by Varden Plas, a leading coachworking firm of Belgium. It has been restored by McKenzie of England, the leading renovator and modifier of all old Bentley cars. Only 1,635 of the 3-Litres were produced and few have survived. Its 4 cylinders are cast en bloc, have integral cylinder heads; the engine is water cooled and develops 80 to 82 m.p.h.

CONTINUED

1926 3-LITRE BENTLEY

1930 6.5-LITRE BENTLEY

1939 BENTLEY

On the heels of the 3-Litre came the 4.5-Litre Bentley, an enormous, heavy sports and touring car. With a massive supercharger, the modest 125 horsepower of this car could be boosted to 175 horsepower for normal use and 240 for racing purposes. It was this model that won at Le Mans in 1928, 1929 and 1930. In fact, in 1929 four Bentleys were fielded and came across the finishing line first, second, third and fourth.

By 1926, Bentley had increased his engine size again, this time to 6 litres. The 6.5-litre car was built from 1926 to 1930. Of the five hundred thirty-nine models produced, one hundred seventy-one were known as Speed Sixes, and it was these models that won at Le Mans in 1929 and 1930. The Speed Six in the Cunningham collection is also a competition model and was, in its day, a known racer. The car's fabric-covered body is light, but the automobile as a whole weighs 4,511 pounds, heavy for a sports or racing car. Yet the car's reliability and its ability to reach high speeds compensated for its weight on the circuit. The Speed Six's engine displays one unusual detail, introduced by W. O. Bentley; its camshafts are driven by cranks, not by the customary gears or chains.

All through these years and despite the successes in racing and the popularity of the car, company finances were shaky. Bentley was a perfectionist and his cars cost money to make and money to buy. Their prices, with body, could reach $13,000.

Just before Bentley Motors Ltd. went into receivership in 1931 he produced an 8-litre car, perhaps as a farewell challenge. It is one of the largest-engined automobiles made after the first World War.

With acquisition by Rolls-Royce, the whole character of the car altered. It became a sedate luxury car, its sporting nature discarded forever. With the exception of the radiator design, the Bentleys made by Rolls-Royce were indistinguishable from the parent automobile.

The Museum has a splendid example of the Rolls Bentley. Its 6-cylinder engine has detachable, pushrod-operated valves. Like the Rolls-Royce, it has servo brakes.

What puts this car into a superior category among vintage automobiles is its coachwork, which was executed by James Young of England. In 1951 this car and seven others were chosen by New York's Museum of Modern Art as exemplars of outstanding automobile design. The razor-edge definition of the roof lines and of the trunk merge and flow into the sweeping curves of the fenders to achieve a single, harmonious whole. The large trunk in the rear has been integrated into the body with such subtlety that its massiveness is barely perceptible. By milling the windshield corner posts out of bar stock, the designer achieved an understated delicacy.

1934 2.3-LITRE ALFA ROMEO

THE 1934 ALFA ROMEO

Like a flash of vivid red, the Alfa Romeo automobile raced across the landscape of the 1920's and the troubled 1930's to claim an enduring and preeminent place in the saga of the sports car. In speed and performance, it held its own against many a Mercedes and Bugatti. In 1924 Alfa Romeos won the European Grand Prix and came in first, second and third in the Italian. A decade of victories was to follow.

The Alfa Romeo began life in a small town outside Milan in the year 1910, under the name Alfa (the initials deriving from the company's name, Anonima Lombardo Fabbrica Automobili). The romantic Romeo was added in 1915 when, prosaically, the small company was absorbed by a bigger one owned by a wealthy industrialist, Nicola Romeo. Shortly after the close of World War I, the company began producing its first cars, essentially the model made before 1914. But very soon—the prototypes were shown in 1921—the firm branched out into a new, more modern 6-cylinder engine design, which incorporated overhead valves and a detachable cylinder head. This car was to make Alfa Romeo famous. By 1925, the car was already World Champion, and the next series produced won every major race in Europe between 1928 and 1930: every one

except the grueling 24-hour Le Mans endurance test, and even there the company was to be vindicated by its next model, the 2.3-Litre.

For four years, from 1931 to 1934, this Alfa Romeo took first place at Le Mans, a spectacular achievement. In 1935 it came in second. To add even more luster to the name, it won the Italian Mille Miglia in 1932, '33 and '34, and came in first, second and third in the Belgian Grand Prix of '32 and '33. Not only speed but endurance were tested by these races, and the victories confirmed that the 2.3-Litre Alfa Romeo had a surplus of both these qualities, so necessary in a sports car.

The supercharged, double overhead cam straight engine of this car developed 142 horsepower and achieved a speed of 105-plus miles per hour. Only one hundred eighty-eight of these expensive cars were made in four years. Some were built with short chassis, some with long. The model in the Cunningham collection is a short chassis. Not only the engine but the long flowing lines of the body, designed by the custom body designing firm Touring make this one of the most treasured exhibits in the Museum, a matchless combination of performance and aesthetics.

THE 1933 PACKARD

Born in Ohio and raised in Detroit—such a geographical geneology may seem unlikely for a car beloved of kings and rajahs, of generals and Communist dictators; yet the world over, not just in the United States alone, the Packard was bought and treasured by the prominent and the well-to-do. Tsar Nicholas owned one, fitted with skis to replace the front wheels for driving on Russian winter roads. General Pershing travelled in a Packard in France during the first World War. Colonel Lindbergh sat in one during his ticker-tape parade up Fifth Avenue in 1927. Josef Stalin admired the Packard so much that he acquired body dies from the company and had the 1945 Russian Z.I.S. copied from them. And the most complimentary gesture of all came from the great Ettore Bugatti himself. When he was forced to take a long trip, he drove a Packard in preference to one of his own cars.

The birth of the Packard was the result, so the story goes, of the dissatisfaction felt by engineer James Ward Packard of Warren, Ohio, for his Winton. Annoyed with its constant breakdowns, he complained to the car's maker, Alexander Winton, and was told to try building one himself. The upshot was that on November 6, 1899, the first Packard, a single-cylinder car which could attain speeds of 40 m.p.h., was

1933 PACKARD PHAETON

produced by James and his brother. From that time on, the company climbed steadily upward until, meeting reverses after World War II, it finally closed its doors in the mid-1950's. By 1903, when the Packard Motor Car Company moved to Detroit, 4-cylinder cars were being made and sold — for $7,500. In 1916 it produced a revolutionary 12-cylinder car, the Twin Six, which was kept in production for seven years. Ralph De Palma set a speed record of a fraction under 150 m.p.h. in an especially built model of the Twin Six.

The Packard Company's reputation for reliability, design and precision in its production was such that, in both world wars, it built engines for airplanes, ships and naval speed boats. The Spitfires flew with Packard-made Rolls-Royce Merlin engines and PT boats were powered by them.

A very special automobile was the 12-cylinder car made from 1931 to 1934. These cars were, to all intents and purposes, hand fitted and assembled, and only sold with custom-made or at least half custom-made bodies. The 1933 model of this car, which stands in the Cunningham collection, a true eye-catcher, was on display in Philadelphia in the spring of 1933. It exemplifies much of what made Packard cars so desirable. A luxurious sports phaeton (a term for an open tourer), the car

has smoothness and flexibility, superior braking power and — for that time — very light steering, especially for such a large piece of machinery.

It is worth taking note of the ingenious design of the rear windshield. The graceful wind-wings are hinged to the windshield and attached at the handle end of the rear doors. Thus they operate with the opening and closing of these doors. However, if passengers riding in the back wanted to eliminate the windshield, they could unhook the wings, place them flat against the windshield and then wind down wings and windshield until they had disappeared completely into the car's dividers. They would then be riding in a perfect flush-deck phaeton.

Credit for the design of this car's body goes to Roy Dietrich, who endowed it with its elegant flowing lines, so noticeably satisfying and achieved without the use of meritricious chrome mouldings. The line of the cockpit was based on the cockpit design of a World War I fighter plane. A unity of compound curves, crisp edges and a striking economy of line make this an exceptionally handsome car, a tribute to the great name it carries.

THE DUESENBERGS

Jimmy Murphy, behind the wheel of a Duesenberg, was the first American driver in an American car ever to win the French Grand Prix. His record stood for forty-six years. It happened on July 25, 1921, at the first French Grand Prix held in seven years. As in the previous Grand Prix of 1914, the French were confident of victory. Once again they were to be disappointed. The Duesenbergs fielded a team of four 3-litres cars, streamlined, sleek and with eye-catching Stars and Stripes painted on the tails of their white bodies.

This particular race has become famous in Grand Prix history—aside from the American upset—for the appallingly bad road surface. Careful preparations had been made but they proved useless. The drivers were blinded by dust; their cars kicked up loose stones, which injured them, their mechanics and automobiles alike.

Murphy, who had broken his ribs during a practice accident, drove in pain and encased in a plaster cast. He, too, suffered from the flying stones. ". . . the tension and the thrill of battle remained until the very end," wrote the English Grand Prix historian Rex Hays in his book, *The Vanishing Litres*, "for when Jimmy Murphy in the 3-litre Duesenberg crossed the line, his radiator was empty and had been so for the last ten minutes of the race, a stone having holed it, and his offside rear tyre was flat."*

Murphy completed the 321.78 circuit in 4 hours, 7 minutes and 11⅔ seconds. He averaged 78.1 m.p.h. and drove one lap at 84 m.p.h. The race was a triumph for America and, of course, for the Duesenberg racing car. Already famous on the racing circuit back home, this victory brought worldwide recognition to the marque.

Fred S. and August S. Duesenberg were two Iowa boys with very little formal education but who became exceptional although self-taught engineers. Their designs and automotive developments contributed substantially to the growth of the car in this country. Their very name has entered the language. "It's a doozy" derives from the great acclaim accorded their cars in the 1920's and 1930's. Above all, the brothers cherished the racing car. They began, in the early years of the century, by building 2-cylinder racing bicycles, turned briefly to heavy farm machinery but, by 1907, had built their first car with a 2-cylinder engine. This last quickly developed into a 4-cylinder car designed specifically for racing.

During the first decade the Duesenbergs worked in Des Moines, financed by a local lawyer whose name, Mason, was given the cars. Masons competed in numerous events, from endurance tests to straight speed races. Barney Oldfield drove them, as did Eddie Rickenbacker. When Mason sold out his interest to Maytag, the washing machine company, the Duesenbergs left, too independent minded to suffer the anonymity of a large company. During the war the brothers, now in New Jersey, built sturdy, durable marine engines for the Navy, as well as producing the Bugatti aero-engine. Unlike so many, the Duesenbergs did not profiteer from war contracts and were forced to sell their company in 1918. They moved back to Des Moines, formed the Duesenberg Motor Company and returned to their greatest interest, the racing car. For the first time, the cars they built raced under the name Duesenberg.

*Rex Hays, *The Vanishing Litres*, (New York, Macmillan Company, 1957), p. 32.

1929 DUESENBERG RACER

They were to garner many honors on the racing circuit. Aside from Murphy's spectacular win, a Duesenberg won the 300-mile Elgin race in 1919; one year later Duesenbergs came in third and fourth in the Indianapolis 500, and in 1924, 1925 and 1927 they came in first. In 1920 one of the brothers' cars, mounted with two straight 8, overhead cam engines with valves-in-head, also set a land speed record of 156.14 m.p.h. at Daytona Beach.

The 1929 racing car in the Cunningham collection is, in all probability, the last car built by the Duesenbergs, which they intended for racing alone. Its engine is fitted with a "side-winder" centrifugal supercharger and an intercooler manifold. The supercharger is mechanically driven at five times engine speed and it rotates the huge "8" impeller at 37/40,000 revolutions per minute. This car was driven by the famous racing driver Fred Frame, who also installed large cylinder blocks and a stroked crankshaft to bring the straight 8 engine size up from its original 91 cubic inches to 168 cubic inches. This engine is an example of workmanship that is breathtaking in the beauty of its mechanical execution. Whereas the chassis of this car is a replacement of the original, the engine stands now as it did when it was built.

In the early 1920's the Duesenberg brothers embarked on the production of a high-priced luxury passenger car known as the Model A. On this car, they were the first to introduce hydraulically operated front wheel brakes to America. The Model A was followed by the Model J and ultimately the Models SJ and SSJ. With these cars the Duesenbergs stole the spotlight from any other American automobile for luxury, speed, safety and dependability. A Duesenberg, without even trying, could pass any other passenger car on the road. The prominent, the glamorous and the merely rich took the Duesenberg to their hearts. Jimmy Walker, Mayor of New York and the 1920's Number One playboy, owned one. So did Elizabeth Arden, Tommy Manville, and the movie star heroes Clark Gable and Gary Cooper. Abroad, these super-luxury cars were also possessions of great cachet: the kings of Italy and of Spain bought them, and rajahs fitted out their Duesenbergs with priceless oriental rugs.

In 1926, the Model J replaced the Model A. At the same time, the ambitious automobile empire builder Erret Loban Cord acquired the company and gave the brothers a free hand to produce a prestige car.

The Model J in the Museum is painted a striking Chinese Red combined with a near black, dark maroon or mulberry color. Only the sunlight, striking on the deep, highly finished polish of the body—designed by Le Baron—brings out the subtlety of the darker red. A light red striping patterns the fenders of this dual cowl phaeton, whose design is accepted as one of the most beautiful among all great classic cars. The interior follows the same color scheme. The upholstery, in leather, and the carpeting throughout the car are both red. As a finishing touch, the rear window glass is bevilled.

The engine of this striking car is a double overhead camshaft straight 8 of 6.9 litres, at a horsepower of 265.

CONTINUED

1930 DUESENBERG MODEL J

The Model SSJ, which was built in 1935, was a short wheelbase roadster. Clark Gable owned one, and Gary Cooper owned the car now in the Cunningham collection. Cooper bought it to vindicate himself. In a previous Duesenberg he had raced — and been beaten by — Groucho Marx behind the wheel of a Mercedes SSK. This unofficial, impromptu race took place in the dry lakes area of California. With his SSJ model, Cooper requested a rematch, got it and won.

The dashboard on the SSJ, which resembles a sophisticated instrument panel, is an engineer's delight. As well as such commonplace devices as a gas gauge and a speedometer, the driver can check on the condition of his engine by an array of indicators: a gauge for manifold pressure and brake pressure, an altimeter, a light that switches on when the chassis gives itself an automatic lubrication and another light that indicates the level of water in the battery. The 7.4 supercharged straight 8 engine is of heroic proportions. It has 4 valves per cylinder and is capable of 400 horsepower.

This very model is one of the last cars built by the Duesenberg brothers. In 1937 the Cord empire collapsed and brought down with it one of the great American marques.

1935 DUESENBERG MODEL SSJ

THE 1934 MG

The initials MG stand for Morris Garages, the place where the original MG Midget was coaxed into being in the early 1920's. Cecil Kimber, general manager of the Oxford branch of the flourishing Morris Motors Ltd., thought he could produce a small car with a big performance potential using standard Morris parts. The result was the first MG, a car with an engine of 4 cylinders, overhead valves and a mere 20 horsepower. Nonetheless, the Midget was quickly awarded a Gold Medal in England's Land's End Trials. One of the world's most favored and successful sports car marques was on its way.

The first Midgets bred the larger Magnettes, which were produced in the early 1930's. As it was a competition model, specifically designed for racing, only thirty-one were made. The car was powered by a 6-cylinder overhead camshaft supercharged engine. Just after it was built, it made the fastest time of day at one section of the Monte Carlo Rally; and it won the Ulster Tourist Trophy in 1933, with the temperamental, brilliant Italian driver Tazio Novulari at the wheel.

The model in the Cunningham Museum was once owned by the British racer Charles Martin, who drove it at Brooklands and Le Mans. This car has been completely restored to its original condition.

1934 MG K3 MAGNETTE

THE CUNNINGHAMS

Set in the rich, rolling landscape of northwest France, Le Mans was once a quietly prosperous marketing town, with a history stretching back into medieval times. Today Le Mans plays host to the world's most famous automobile race: Les Ving-quatre Heures du Mans. No other circuit equals it in prestige or in popularity with makers of cars or with spectators. Some 300,000 travel to Le Mans every June to witness the gruelling 24-hour endurance trial. A win at Le Mans is a glorious triumph and all the great marques of the sports-car world have participated, from Alfa Romeos and Bentleys to Bugattis and Stutzes.

The original purpose of the race was to test the reliability and the performance of cars destined for the general public. Entries had to compete with standard road equipment, lights had to function, all repairs had to be carried out by the driver with the standard tools carried in the car and refueling was only permitted at set intervals. As today's average passenger car could not hope to survive the rigors of the circuit, specially built prototypes are now permitted. Cars built specifically as Grand Prix racing machines are still excluded.

Almost from the first race in 1923, American cars competed at the Le Mans circuit, which had been constructed on the site of a World War I American Army base. That first year a competing car, called the Montier Special, was in reality a Model T, entered by Ford's Paris dealer. In 1926 two Overlands and one Willys-Knight, both with modified engines, took part, but neither performed well. American cars put up a good fight in 1928, when a Stutz placed second and two Chryslers took third and fourth place. The successful drivers, however, were French. In 1934 and in 1935 a Duesenberg, owned by Rumanian royalty, competed with no exceptional results. In the last year before the war ended all European racing, the American sports-car enthusiast Miles Collier drove his specially built MG Midget at Le Mans. Eight hours after the start a split fuel tank put the MG out of commission. It was the fifteenth Le Mans race (because of general political and industrial unrest one had been cancelled in 1936) and still no American driver in an American car had come close to winning.

During the war years Le Mans was once again put to military use. The RAF was stationed there before the fall of France; then the Luftwaffe built new runways, which became, inevitably, a target for Allied bombers. At war's end Le Mans's famous circuit was a shamble of bomb craters and destroyed buildings. Not until 1949 was the track once again in running gear.

Regulations were somewhat altered after the war. While windshields, fenders and other appurtenances of the sports car were still required, two-seaters with streamlined bodies were now permitted to compete. Each lap was shortened by some two miles to measure 8.36 miles. Certain minimum speeds were set to which cars of specified engine capacity had to conform, and refueling was only permitted every 234.7 miles. Once

again, however, only tools carried in the automobile were allowed for repairs.

The desire, among American racing enthusiasts, for an American win at Le Mans was intense. National pride was at stake here, as well as the feeling that the world's leading producer of cars should bid for the glory of winning the world's leading race. Briggs Swift Cunningham—yachtsman, sportsman and amateur racing driver—took the lead in the American thrust to win at Le Mans. To count, the victory had to go to an American driver behind the wheel of an American-built car.

From 1950 to 1955 Briggs Cunningham, the cars he built and the drivers he chose battled the top-ranking marques—Ferraris, Jaguars, Aston Martins among them—for first place at Le Mans. While total victory always eluded the Cunningham teams, their performance brought credit and esteem to American sports cars. In 1949 Cunningham entered two Cadillacs, the biggest machines to be seen at Le Mans since the Bentleys and the Mercedes SSK's of the early 1930's. Because of its size, one Cadillac was nicknamed *Le Monstre*. It says much for the performance of these cars that they lasted the entire 24 hours and that, among sixty entries, they finished tenth and eleventh.

For the next year's race, Cunningham elected to build and enter cars made by himself. In a small workshop in West Palm Beach, Florida, he and his helpers were to produce a series of sports cars designated as a C-1R through a C-6R. Of these cars it was the C-4R that turned in the most impressive performance. In 1952 Briggs Cunningham, doing most of the 24-hour driving himself, brought his car into a fourth-place win. One of his other entries suffered valve failure; another got stuck in a sandbank. The following year all three Cunningham cars were numbered among the first ten finishers, a C-5 roadster came in third, the C-4R seventh and the C-4 coupe arrived tenth.

The C-5R was the fastest car at Le Mans. It was clocked at 154.88 m.p.h. through the circuit's flying kilometer. It also earned the nickname the "Smiling Shark" from the French spectators because of its radiator grille which curls up at each end. In 1954 two C-4R's competed once again and finished third and fourth.

The C-4R, the most successful of the Cunningham models used in sports-car racing, is powered by a V-8 Chrysler hemi engine of 5.4 litres. Four carburetor intake manifolds (a later version used four Weber down-draft double throat units), tubular frames with De Dion suspension on the rear and 4-speed ZF gearboxes, all contributed to making this machine a highly competitive model. A huge cooler is mounted in the air stream on top of the body cowling on the right-hand side. The C-4RK, an offshoot of the C-4R, is a coupe, whose body was designed by Dr. W. Kamm (the K honors him). His theories of aerodynamics favored a blunt rear section in opposition to the customary long-tailed rear section.

1955 was to be the last year of the Cunningham cars. This was the year of great tragedy at Le Mans. Much has been written and every half-second of the disastrous accident has been analyzed to determine why it happened. Whatever the cause, the result was the death of a driver and the deaths of over eighty spectators. It was racing history's greatest catastrophe. Although the race was not called off—a Jaguar won—the accident cast a black shadow over Le Mans that year. Cunningham's C-6R, which carried an Offenhauser engine, turned in a weak performance and retired with a broken piston.

Despite great promise, no outright triumph had come to the American team. The West Palm Beach workshop was closed and the next time Briggs Cunningham came to Le Mans, in 1960, it was to be with an American Corvette. Victory came in 1967, when A. J. Foyt and Dan Gurney, two Americans, brought an MK IV Ford first across the finish line.

CUNNINGHAM C-5R   FOLLOWING PAGES: CUNNINGHAM C-4R

1952 GRAND PRIX TALBOT-LAGO

THE 1952 TALBOT-LAGO
THE 1948 FERRARI
THE 1967 FERRARI
THE 1954 MASERATI
THE 1967 LAMBORGHINI
THE 1958 REVENTLOW
SCARAB

The second World War was hardly over and most of Europe still in ruins when automobile racing was resumed. In the summer of 1946 a race—the Grand Prix des Nations—was staged in Geneva, the circuit running in the shadow of the League of Nations' Palais des Nations. The cars were the old familiar favorites, hastily prepared pre-war models that had survived the wreckages of war. The Alfa Romeos, it was reported, had spent the years skillfully concealed in a cheese factory. It was, in fact, this marque that was to dominate European racing for the next five years until, in the early 1950's, it was challenged by the Italian Ferrari and Maserati and the Talbot-Lago, a car which, although manufactured in France, owed its existence to the talented Italian automobile designer Antony Lago.

CONTINUED

1958 REVENTLOW SCARAB

1967 LAMBORGHINI P-400 MUIRA

1954 GRAND PRIX MASERATI

The mixed ancestry of the Talbot-Lago—part British, part French—is too complex to disentangle; but it has led to a confusion of names, so that the car is sometimes called a Lago-Talbot and occasionally a mere Talbot, a name which does not pay its dues to the car's creator. Major Antony Lago, Venetian by birth, had gone to England after the first World War where he worked for the British automobile industry. In 1933 he was dispatched to France to revive the ailing French brand of a British firm. Within two years he took over the branch—now divorced from its English partner—and achieved his ambition, to design and produce fast and luxurious cars. Tony Lago's passion was racing and the Talbot-Lago competed and won laurels in many major events before the war. In 1937, Lago's team placed first, second and third in the French Grand Prix. In England's Tourist Trophy his team came in first and second and in two lesser but nonetheless significant events, the Grand Prix at Marseilles and at Tunis, Lago's racers won again. As a result of these successes, Lago's sports cars and other models began to sell.

With the fall of France in 1940, automobile production ceased. Lago, as an Italian national, escaped German expropriation. When war ended, he could resume manufacture without the handicaps of some others whose plants had been destroyed or facilities worn out by war production. He began almost immediately to make passenger and racing cars, using a pre-war 4.5-litre engine. On the racing circuit, despite fierce competition from supercharged 1.5-litre Alfa Romeos and Maseratis, his larger, but ruggedly dependable engine, held its own brilliantly. (Since the beginning of Grand Prix and other racing, certain entry specifications, relating to engine size,

have always been set. These are known as formulae.) After the war, in order to make use of as many pre-war racing machines as possible, the Grand Prix formula was expanded to allow 1.5-litre cars, supercharged, to compete in the same race as 4.5-litre cars, unsupercharged. The Alfa Romeo and the Maserati engines commanded more power, but the Talbot-Lagos' lower power had a wider range combined with good suspension and, unsupercharged, the engine consumed much less fuel, thereby requiring fewer time-consuming pit stops. In the first four years after 1945, Antony Lago's cars won the French Grand Prix of 1947, came in second at the Monaco Grand Prix of 1948, won the Belgian and the French again in 1949. In 1950 the car placed first in the 24-hour endurance race at Le Mans.

Despite these achievements and the publicity they garnered for Talbot-Lagos, the marque's car sales diminished. Handsome, exotically designed Gran Turismo sports cars much respected everywhere, their sale was hindered in their native France by the curious French taxation system. Ownership of a luxury automobile was taken as an index of taxability, which meant that few of those who could afford them bought ostentatiously expensive cars. In the export market, Tony Lago met fierce competition from other established sports-car marques, like the Jaguars and the Ferraris. In time he was forced to give up designing and building his own engines and make cars with inferior engines from other firms. In 1957, in one last attempt to survive, he made the Lago America for the American market. It, too, failed commercially. In 1958 Antony Lago sold his company to the large Simca complex. One year later he died.

The magnificent memorial to his name that stands in the

1948 2-LITRE FERRARI, 166 SPYDER CORSA

Cunningham Museum was built in 1952. Its 6-cylinder engine is rated at 280 horsepower, its massive wheels and chassis weigh in at nearly 2,000 lbs. Yet, despite its giant wheels and its weight, the car's excellent suspension makes it easy to manage. Seated behind the wheel in the cockpit, the driver's feet are set widely apart, on either side of the engine, thus providing him with good lateral bracing in moments of hard cornering. Over the years, this stolid, good-natured Talbot-Lago has gained the affection and respect of many drivers.

To many of those whose concerns embrace the automobile, the cars made by Enzo Ferrari of Modena, Italy, are unmatched anywhere in the world today. This splendid name is carried on racing cars, sports cars and passengers cars. All are expensive. A present-day Ferrari costs between $32,000 and $35,000, with the most expensive model running as high as $75,000. Not many are made at such prices but such is their reputation that they sell.

From the first Enzo Ferrari loved racing and every car he makes owes a debt to his racing machines. Beginning in the 1920's, Ferrari was a test driver, a mechanic and, briefly, a racing driver. It was during his racing days that he adopted his conspicuous emblem, the prancing black horse. It had been the ensignia of a fallen Italian World War I air ace.

Ferrari was not an outstandingly successful driver himself; his true talents lay in organizing. In 1929 he founded the Scuderia Ferrari, a stable which managed Alfa Romeo's racing cars. It was under Ferrari's talented direction—he picked the drivers and organized the back-up pit work—that the Alfa Romeos came to the forefront in racing history. In 1938 Alfa Romeo severed its ties with Ferrari, and he now turned to the production of racing cars that would carry his own name. War intervened—he became a machine tool manufacturer for the duration—but in 1945 Enzo Ferrari produced the first genuine Ferrari. This landmark automobile was designed by Gioacchino Colombo, who had worked with great success for Alfa Romeo. The car was first made with a 1.5-litre engine, which was quickly increased to 2 litres. It came in three models: a coupe to carry passengers, a sports car and a competition model. Among two hundred entries, this car won the Mille Miglia and the Tour of Sicily in 1948. The following year the Ferrari was the winner at the first post-war 24-hour Le Mans race.

The 2-litre 166 Ferrari in the Museum is the sports-car version of this successful competition model. This particular car was the first Ferrari to be brought over to the United States, where it was raced by Briggs Cunningham in numerous road events. Its V-12 engine produces a remarkable 160 horsepower when it is tuned to burn alcohol. The body of this early Ferrari model gives no hint of the Ferrari body designs to come, which are renowned for the sculptured look of their aluminum sheathing. In contrast, the styling of the 166 is spartan and utilitarian, with barely perceptible streamlining. But the engine and the chassis were to become the cornerstone of all subsequent Ferrari cars.

Throughout the 1950's and 1960's Ferrari racing achievements became legendary—and did much to sell his excessively expensive cars. Among other victories, a Ferrari won the 12-hour Sebring race in 1956; a year later Ferrari took first and second place in the Mille Miglia. It was a tragic race, for one Ferrari crashed, killing the driver, a passenger and twelve spectators. Thereafter, the Mille Miglia—which had been run from Brescia to Rome and back—was transformed into a safer, albeit less challenging, rally. The next year, 1958, Ferraris won again at Sebring, took Le Mans and the Targa Florio race in Sicily. In 1962 and the three following years, Enzo Ferrari's cars won Le Mans. In 1966 Ferrari came in first at the Belgian and then the French Grand Prix. In this last race, the Ferrari marked the sixtieth anniversary of the first Grand Prix of 1906 by doubling exactly the average fastest lap speed of 63 m.p.h. of the original Grand Prix winner.

Side by side with his competition cars, Ferrari built sports models throughout the 1960's. These were, in effect, detuned versions of his racers. The second Ferrari in the Museum—the 1967 275 GTB/4—is an exciting, high-performance road machine. It is powered by a 12-cylinder, 60° V engine of 3.28-litres, which has an output of 280 horsepower and reaches speeds of 170 m.p.h. The number "4" in the car's designation stands for the engine's four overhead camshafts. This car is front-engined, unlike Ferrari's competition models of the 1960's, which were already rear-engined. In 1958, he built his first rear-engined car, the Dino, named after his son Alfredino, who had died of leukemia two years earlier. In the early 1960's he also made a sports car, the 4.9-litre Superfast, which sold for $24,400 and was at the time the most expensive car in the world.

Unlike Ferrari, who did not make cars until after the war, the name Maserati goes back to the beginning days of automobile racing. It all began, in the earliest years of the century, with five Italian brothers: Alfieri, Ernesto, Carlo, Bindo and Ettore. All five were racing maniacs, men who loved the automobile. Brother Carlo, for instance, raced the now-forgotten Bianchi in the German Kaiserpreis of 1907. Alfieri worked for Isotta Fraschini. Then, in 1914, the brothers—without Carlo, who died in 1910—opened a small garage in Bologna. War came and they kept the business alive by making spark plugs; but as soon as they could, they returned to racing, modifying and rebuilding other people's makes into special

CONTINUED

racing machines. By 1926 they had made a car built entirely by themselves. With Alfieri driving, it won the Targa Florio. For the next few years, the Fratelli Maserati specialized in designing and constructing racing cars and hand-built automobiles for very special customers. In 1932 Alfieri died. In this country, the American racing driver Wilbur Shaw brought a 3-litre, straight-8 Maserati into first place at Indianapolis, the first European car to win there in twenty years. In 1940 Shaw won the same race a second time, once again with a Maserati.

The Maserati brothers, always on the verge of bankruptcy, were absorbed by a large Italian firm shortly before the second World War. Once the war was over, they continued to make expensive sports and competition cars, eventually going out on their own again. They left their famous name behind and their future cars were known as Oscas. Their greatest single victory — after placing well but not outstandingly at Le Mans and in the Mille Miglia race — was at Sebring in the 12-hour race of 1954. Entered by Briggs Cunningham and driven by the English ace driver Sterling Moss with Bill Lloyd, the Osca came in to win ahead of much larger cars.

The 250F model in the Cunningham collection is a highly successful Maserati, built in 1954 to the 2.5-litre Grand Prix formula. It was, with this particular 250F, that the famous Argentinian racing driver Juan Manuel Fangio won his fifth World Championship in 1957. Whereas most Grand Prix automobiles have engines with cylinders based on multiples of four, the 250F is one of the few 6-cylinder cars to achieve Grand Prix fame. Its 2.5-litre double overhead camshaft engine is not only potent but also reliable. This Maserati was one of the last racing machines designed for the Grand Prix that placed the engine in front of the driver. Very shortly after 1954, Grand Prix car engines were put behind the driver for greater power; they have remained there ever since. Apart from performance, the aesthetics of this car contribute to its reputation as one of the highest ranking of all post-war Italian machines. Many experts maintain it is the most beautifully proportioned Italian racing car ever built.

Throughout the 1960's, in Italy as elsewhere, car manufacturers began to specialize to a greater extent and sports cars were designed and built that were never intended as com-

petition cars. The curious result is that some of the fastest, best-performing cars today have never been linked to the racing circuit. Among these are the automobiles built by Ferruccio Lamborghini.

Lamborghini began working shortly after the war tuning Fiat 500's. But by 1949 he had started his own business, building tractors, largely from Allied surplus war machinery. By the mid-1960's he was a very prosperous manufacturer of heavy equipment, mostly agricultural. When he branched out into automobiles—more perhaps as a hobby than as a moneymaker—he took for his emblem a bull. If, as some say, this was a challenge to Ferrari's aristocratic black horse, it became an effective one. By 1965 two hundred Lamborghinis were on the market and competing very successfully with Ferraris.

The Lamborghini P-400, built in 1967, is capable of speeds up to 170 m.p.h. Its 3.9-litre V-12 engine produces an admirable 396 horsepower. Its acceleration—from 0 to 60 m.p.h. in a range of 7 to 8 seconds—matches that of any fast road car ever made. The model, known as the "Muira", which stands in the Cunningham Museum, is the epitome of luxury, elegance and comfort as well. The interior is carpeted in deep white pile which complements the shimmering, mother-of-pearl exterior paint. The windows go up and down electrically. This car is the personal property of Mrs. Laura Cunningham, at one time a racing driver herself.

Lance Reventlow, heir to the Woolworth fortune through his mother, Barbara Hutton, was killed in a plane crash in 1972. But before his death he built top-performing cars that considerably advanced the design and engineering of the American competition car. It can be said that Reventlow took over in the 1960's the pioneer work done in the '50's by Briggs Cunningham. One of Reventlow's cars, built to the design of Leo Goossen, incorporated the advanced concept of desmodromic valves. These function without the use of valve springs, instead opening and closing mechanically. After Reventlow's death, his custom-built cars were donated to the Cunningham Museum. The 1958 Scarab—so named after the Egyptian beetle—has a 350-cubic-inch, V-8 Chevrolet engine, which was modified for racing purposes.

1967 FERRARI 275 GTB/4

This close-up view of the left-hand side of a 1929 Duesenberg racing engine—perhaps the last one built—reveals a fine finned inter-cooler manifold and a "side-winder" super-charger. The displacement of the straight-8 engine was initially 91 cubic inches; it was twice increased and now, by the installation of a new stroked crankshaft, displaces 168.5 cubic inches.

INDEX

 ALFA ROMEO

 DELAGE

Visible in the right-hand view of this same
engine are its timing gear tower, double
overhead camshafts, forward-mounted water
pump and manifold. Behind the water pump
lie the drive shaft and right-angle "one-to-
one" drive for the supercharger. The fine
precision workmanship of the engine as a
whole transforms it from mere machinery
into an example of automotive sculpture at
its best.